MW01204820

How To Go *Almost* Anywhere For *Almost* Nothing

by
Maureen A. Hennessy

Writers Club Press

San Jose · New York · Lincoln · Shanghai

How To Go Almost Anywhere for Almost Nothing

Copyright © 1999 Maureen A. Hennessy

This book may not be reproduced or distributed, in whole or in part, in print or by any other means without the written permission of the author. You can contact the author at: GOMH@aol.com.

ISBN: 1-893652-49-1

Library of Congress Catalog Card Number: 99-66005

This book was published using the on-line/on-demand publishing services of Writers Club Press, an imprint of iUniverse, Inc.

iUniverse.com, Inc.
620 North 48th Street
Suite 201
Lincoln NE 68504-3467
www.iUniverse.com

URL: http://www.writersclub.com

TABLE OF CONTENTS

INTRODUCTION   1
PART ONE: GETTING THERE   3
CHAPTER ONE: AIR TRAVEL: 3
COURIER FLIGHTS   3
ON-BOARD COURIER FLIGHT   3
USA ORIGINATING COURIER FLIGHTS   4
WHAT IS AN ON-BOARD COURIER?   4
REQUIREMENTS OF AN
ON-BOARD COURIER   5
WHAT ARE THE RESTRICTIONS?   6
CHANGING YOUR ITINERARY   7
OTHER REQUIREMENTS AND
RESPONSIBILITIES   8
THE FIRST TRIP   9
SOME SPECIFIC COURIER COMPANIES   11
FREQUENT FLYER MILEAGE   13
PROMOTIONAL FLIGHTS AND CRUISES   14
FREE FLIGHTS   15
COUPON BROKERS   16
CHARTER AIRLINES   16
STATUS FARES   17
CHILDREN/INFANT/STUDENT FARES   17
BEREAVEMENT FARES   19
SENIOR FARES   19
BUCKET SHOPS   20
GETTING BUMPED   21
GROUND TRANSPORTATION,
NORTH AMERICA   22
TRAIN AND BUS   22
AUTO DRIVEAWAY   23
PART TWO: NOW I'M HERE, NOW WHAT?   26
BUDGET HOUSING, WORLDWIDE   26

YOUTH HOSTELS	26
DISCOUNT TRAVEL CLUBS	28
HOSTEL ALTERNATIVES, WORLDWIDE	29
RELIGIOUS RETREATS	29
COLLEGES AND UNIVERSITIES	30
SPECIAL PLACES - UNITED STATES	31
PORTLAND, OREGON	31
SEEING THE SITES	31
GETTING AROUND	33
WHERE TO STAY-LOW BUDGET	34
MODERATELY PRICED	
HOUSING ALTERNATIVES	35
WHERE TO EAT IN PORTLAND	36
NEW YORK CITY	37
GETTING AROUND	38
NEW YORK CITY BEACHES	39
THE NEIGHBORHOODS	41
NOTEWORTHY	
NEIGHBORHOOD MUSEUMS	42
ACCOMMODATIONS	43
UNIVERSITY AND COLLEGE STAYS	43
HOTELS WITH A DIFFERENCE:	44
HOSTELS:	47
OTHER NEW YORK HOSTELS	50
PASSPORT HOSTELS	50
EATING IN NEW YORK	51
STUFF YOU CAN DO FOR	
FREE IN THE BIG APPLE	52
CALIFORNIA CITIES	53
SAN FRANCISCO	53
GETTING AROUND	54
PLACES TO STAY - BUDGET	55
HOSTELS	55
UNIVERSITIES AND COLLEGES	57
MODERATE COST ACCOMMODATIONS	57

GETTING AROUND	58
BUDGET ACCOMMODATIONS	59
HOSTELS	59
SOME SPECIAL AMERICAN HOSTELS	61
HAWAII	61
OREGON	63
WASHINGTON STATE	63
NEVADA	64
SOME EUROPEAN HOSTELS	65
SCOTLAND	65
IRELAND	66
DUBLIN	67
CORK	68
ENGLAND	69
LONDON AND ENVIRONS	69
ACCOMMODATIONS	71
EATING AND SHOPPING IN GREAT BRITAIN	72
MOROCCO	73
TANGIER – THE JOURNEY BEGINS	74
HELLO AGAIN FROM TANGIER	74
ROUGHING IT IN RABAT	75
CASABLANCA	76
THE MARRAKECH EXPRESS	77
THE MARRAKECH CONFERENCE	79
RETURN TO CASABLANCA	80
TOUJOURS TANGIER	81
TANGIER	82
BACK IN TANGIER	84
THE PIGEON HAS LANDED	85
SIDEBAR – MOROCCO HOSTELS	86
ITALY	87
SOME GENERALITIES	87
ACCOMMODATIONS	88
DINING IN ITALY	88
ROME	89

SPECIAL PLACES, ASIA   92
SINGAPORE   92
HOUSING IN SINGAPORE   93
SIGHTSEEING   95
EATING IN SINGAPORE   96
SHOPPING IN SINGAPORE   98
GETTING AROUND   99
MALAYSIA   101
GETTING THERE   102
HOUSING   103
MELAKA   104
HOUSING IN MELAKA   105
PENANG   105
EATING IN PENANG   106
KUALA LUMPUR   106
HOUSING IN KUALA LUMPUR   107
GENTING HIGHLANDS   108
SHOPPING IN MALAYSIA   108
EATING IN MALAYSIA   109
RUNNING IN MALAYSIA   110
THAILAND   110
KOH SAMUI   111
KOH SAMUI HOUSING AND FOOD   112
EATING IN THAILAND   113
SHOPPING IN THAILAND   113
BANGKOK   115
CHIANG MAI   115
GETTING TO AND AROUND CHIANG MAI   116
SHOPPING IN CHIANG MAI   117
HOUSING IN CHIANG MAI   118
EATING IN CHIANG MAI   118
HONG KONG   119
HOUSING   121
LANTAU ISLAND   124
SHOPPING IN HONG KONG   125

RECREATION AND
ENTERTAINMENT IN HONG KONG   127
EATING IN HONG KONG   129
MACAU   131
EATING IN MACAU   134
SECTION THREE   135
SOME GENERAL TIPS FOR
THE BUDGET TRAVELER   135
PACKING FOR YOUR TRIP   135
MONETARY MATTERS   137
OBTAINING FOREIGN CURRENCY   137
USING CREDIT CARDS   139
HOW MUCH MONEY SHALL I BRING?   140
ILLNESS   141
THE DREADED JET LAG   143
SAFETY AND SECURITY   145
SOME GENERAL CONSIDERATIONS   148
SOLO TRAVEL OR TEAMING UP   148
BEST TIMES TO TRAVEL   149

APPENDIX A: AIR COURIER COMPANIES   150
APPENDIX B   152
BUDGET TRAVEL GUIDES   152
ABOUT THE AUTHOR   155

Introduction:

I always looked forward to a time when I would have the time, opportunity and money to travel. When I finally had the time, my finances were, to say the least, limited. I had worked for years at a career that required travel, but traveling on an expense account is poor preparation for the real world where you have to pay the bills. I knew about hotels at all price levels because in one job I paid my own expenses and tried to economize. Most cheap big-city hotels I found were glorified flophouses located in tawdry surroundings where I felt a real necessity to barricade myself in my room from dusk to dawn. Some of them featured nighttime sounds of screaming, sirens and gunshots, thus negating the need for any "reality" television for entertainment. I had no idea of the many attractive, secure, clean and inexpensive alternatives that exist even in the most expensive cities in the world. You will find many of these listed herein.

Comparison of published airfares was discouraging, and travel agents seem to focus on selling expensive packages, especially to seniors. Disappointed in the "affordable" trips advertised in the media, I still could not despair of fulfilling a lifelong dream of traveling the world, so I began a quest for information on REALLY cheap travel. I researched an extraordinary amount of published material and then embarked upon many years of travel and research in the United States and abroad.

You can judge the results for yourself by all that follows. I have now traveled extensively and at very little expense in Asia, North America, Europe and a bit in Africa. The scope of this particular volume will necessarily focus on areas with which I have the greatest familiarity. Southeast Asia remains a favorite because of the low ground costs, and the most detailed information will cover Asian ports of call such as Hong Kong, Malaysia, Thailand and Singapore, with some reference to specific destinations within Europe and the United States. My latest major trip was to Morocco, and that country is covered in this edition.

In the United States, the largest port of entry cities will get the most attention, not only because three of my favorite cities fall into this category, but for the benefit of visitors from other lands. The principles outlined herein should pertain to travel almost everywhere and you will be able to apply them with just a little bit of courage and imagination.

In the interest of full disclosure, I must admonish the reader that this kind of travel is not for everyone. This is not for the timid or the faint of heart. If you must have luxury, pampering and maid service, see your travel agent. If you are driven to insanity by inefficiency ... if you must have a schedule and the idea of "winging it" frightens you, I recommend you to more conventional travel guides. If, however, you enjoy discovering the unknown and don't mind roughing it a bit, and most of all, if you love a great bargain, by all means read this book. Your reward will be interesting new friends from all over the world and the thrill of discovery of cultures vastly different from your own.

Part One

GETTING THERE

AIR TRAVEL

On-Board Courier Flight

The least expensive mode of air travel involves flying as an on-board courier. There are many companies in major cities worldwide that employ on-board couriers. In American telephone directories, the listing in the yellow pages is usually under the heading, "Air Courier Service", "Courier Service" or something similar. I have listed a number of these companies in Appendix A at the back of this volume. I hasten to add that these companies come and go with regularity, changing ownership or methods of dealing with on-board couriers. In addition to those listed, companies often advertise in major newspapers in San Francisco, Los Angeles and New York. Some companies advertise in the travel section but most advertisements will be found in the classified section under the headings "Tours & Travel", "Transportation" or "Tickets". These usually list several destination cities and a round-trip fare for each. Most of the flights originating in San Francisco and Los Angeles are for various Asian ports, Australia, or London. From New York, your destination can be almost anywhere, and flights originating in Miami generally go to South America. Courier flights originating in London will go virtually everywhere in the world. With careful planning you can continue from London to wherever you want to go regardless of your starting point.

USA Originating Courier Flights

From the West coast typical round trip fares for destinations such as London, Tokyo, Hong Kong, Singapore or Bangkok will cost about $350.00. Sydney, Australia is usually a little more. The traveler is also required to advance a $100.00 or more refundable deposit. This is refunded upon return without delay when you return as scheduled. It is possible to fly for less, occasionally even free, if the traveler is put on the "short list" Once on the "short list", you may get a telephone call requesting a short-notice trip to any of the cities serviced by the company. You may be requested to report to the airport on the very next day, or you may be given as much as a week. This is great for the adventurous, especially those with very flexible schedules.

Most trips departing the West Coast are scheduled for a two-weeks while Australian trips are usually for three-week periods.

Flights that originate on the East Coast seem to vary considerably in duration, from several days to more than thirty days, and the destinations are unlimited. If you want to go to South America, there are lots of flights out of Miami.

What is an On-Board Courier?

An on-board courier flies as a passenger, usually coach class, although, much to my delight, I was "bumped up" to business class on one crowded flight. The baggage space ordinarily available to that passenger is allotted to the courier company for the purpose of shipping goods and/or documents to a recipient in the destination city. You must have a valid passport and, in the case of some destinations, such as Australia, a visa. Your presence is normally required when the Airline company processes the baggage. Don't worry, this is all handled by the representatives of the courier company and is their responsibility. You simply must be physically present during the process. This means being present at the ticket counter in the airport as much as two or three hours before your flight.

Occasionally you will be given a pouch containing documents to be delivered to the company agent in the destination airport. This pouch is to be carried on board with you and you will be given explicit instructions where to go upon arrival to surrender it. Once this is done you are free to go. If you are not given a pouch to deliver, you can make your way through customs with your personal baggage and begin your holiday.

Requirements of an On-Board Courier

An on-board courier must be at least 18 years old, 21 with some companies, and in good health. You must possess a valid passport (and sometimes visa) as required at destination. You need to be suitably attired, as you will represent the courier company. This means no scruffy denims, shorts, etc., and you should look as business-like as is comfortable on a long flight.

If you wish to book a courier flight, you will usually need to give advance notice. How much notice will depend upon the time of year and the company involved. They like to have several months notice when possible, but on occasion you can get the flight you want in as little as a few hours. When you are ready to finalize your travel plans, your flight is booked by telephone. Calling the courier company, you request a specific date. The company can usually accommodate you. The duration of your stay is ordinarily two weeks, although I have on occasion stayed a month at the request of a company when it fit with my plans. Once you have requested a flight by telephone, you will be sent a contract. The contract spells out the details of your flight, your responsibilities and the company's. The signed contract is returned to the company along with your remittance covering your flight, plus deposit. For instance if your destination is Hong Kong and you start from San Francisco, your remittance would usually be $350.00 plus $100.00 deposit. This pays your round-trip fare in full and the deposit is returned upon completion of your trip as long as you have fulfilled your obligations.

What are the Restrictions?

Only one courier can travel on any given flight. This means solo travel. If you want to go with someone, that person will have to book either the day before or the day after your flight. I found that worked very well on the one occasion when I did want someone to vacation with. My friend had never traveled abroad and had never traveled as a courier, so we booked her one day after me. That way, she could go with me to the airport and observe the procedure for departure before actually going through it herself. Then, I could meet her flight when she arrived at destination the next day. The advantages and disadvantages of solo travel will be discussed later on in this book.

You will usually be allowed only carry-on baggage, although some courier companies will also allow one checked bag. Personally, I find the carry-on restriction advantageous. First, it's the fastest way to get out of the airport as you don't have to wait for your bag and, of course, there is less hassle at customs. Traveling with more than you can reasonably carry can be a terrific burden when you get where you are going and can result in unnecessary hassle and expense. For instance, when you arrive in Hong Kong, you can go to Kowloon (where most of the hotels and hostels are located) in several ways. You could take a taxi which would cost about $8.50 U.S., or you can take Bus A-1 for about $1.80 U.S. Muscling lots of luggage on a bus is no fun even when they provide luggage racks up front. Also, many of the hostels are located at some distance from available transportation and it is likely that you will have to do a lot of hiking during your stay. A large, well-balanced backpack is really ideal but remember it must fit in the overhead luggage bins aboard the craft.

Next to a backpack, a suitcase with wheels or a packable suitcase dolly is best. The usefulness of wheeled bags will depend entirely upon the destination. These will work very well in most cities of the United States, where sidewalks are often made to accommodate wheelchairs and mandatory stair climbing is rare. Most of the places I choose to visit render wheeled bags useless because of rutted or cobbled streets, high or irregular curbs and lots of stairs to climb almost everywhere. I have also found it useful to take a daypack for short trips away from my primary destination. That way, you can check your most cumbersome baggage and travel light when you are likely to do a lot of walking. Daypacks are also useful to have with you when shopping some of those great street markets.

Changing Your Itinerary.

Once your contract has been signed and your trip paid for, it is exceedingly difficult to make any changes. If you find you must re-book your trip and you are able to give at least 30 days notice, the company may accommodate you if it is possible. If this is done you will probably be assessed some additional charge.

Cancellation charges apply in the event you must completely give up the trip. The percentage of your payment will depend upon the number of days prior to the flight that the cancellation is made. If you cancel at the last minute or miss your flight, you will probably lose the full amount.

The following is an excerpt from an actual courier contract, which spells out cancellation penalties for one courier company:

Cancellation Notice GivenCancellation Charge

More than 56 daysDeposit or 25% whichever is higher
56 - 30 daysDeposit or 50% whichever is higher
29 - 1 day90%
Day of departure100%

You can see it pays to plan ahead!

Other Requirements and Responsibilities.

You are also responsible for departure taxes on international flights. This tax will range from about $12 to $25. Departure tax from Hong Kong is about $19.00 at the current exchange rate. I believe there is some kind of departure tax at all international airports.

You will be given a detailed sheet of instructions when you depart your origination city. This not only spells out what is expected of you, it will sometimes provide a map of the airports involved in your itinerary. This is very helpful, especially if there is any kind of stopover planned. Some flights may have as much as a 12-hour layover. When this occurs, the company generally arranges for a place for you to rest. As an example, when I have traveled to Singapore via Japan, I was transported by company van to a hotel owned by the airline even when the layover was six hours. The hotel was luxurious and provided some great amenities in the room. There was green tea laid out, a kimono and slippers and a lovely bath provided with all the personal supplies you could want. A note of caution: Meals are *not* provided and you will not want to deal with the prices in Japanese hotels. I had a meager breakfast of coffee and toast at the hotel which set me back $12.00 U.S.! It was the least expensive item on the menu.

Your instructions will include an admonition to contact the company agent in the destination city upon arrival and again 2 or 3 days prior to departure. Contact is made by telephone; and the response (upon arrival) is to welcome you and request a contact telephone number in case the company needs to reach you. The call you make prior to departure will result in instructions regarding that departure.

Other than the above, you may do as you please during your stay - even leave the country if you wish, as long as you return in time to meet your responsibilities to the company. You will be responsible for all of your ground expenses as well as for any expense incurred in getting to the origination airport. There will be much more information to come in future chapters about inexpensive ways to get around once you reach your destination.

The First Trip

The first trip was a little scary. I only had information from one company and that information was quite limited. I wondered if there could be illicit cargo such as drugs or weapons. I could easily conjure up a picture of being arrested and jailed forever in some third world country. This was not the case. That kind of courier company does not do business with respectable airline companies such as Japan Airlines, American, TWA, Singapore Airlines, or United Airlines.

When selecting a destination for my first trip, I thought I'd like some exotic place, something really different from home. This resulted in an in-depth look at Asia. I found the land expenses in Asia considerably less than Europe and the relative strength of the U. S. dollar also made this an attractive prospect. It was difficult to choose; but when I came across Kuala Lumpur on the map the die was cast. Surely this was the most exotic-sounding place in all of Southeast Asia. Additionally, Kuala Lumpur is less than a day's journey from Singapore.

The flight was wonderful and awful. Wonderful because of Singapore Airlines and the newness of a flight abroad. Awful because with layovers in Honolulu (in the wee hours of the morning when nothing was open in the airport) and in Hong Kong (where you are not allowed out of the waiting area) the trip took almost 23 hours. Sleeping was difficult and smoke was a bit of a problem. Cigarette smoke made the recycled air unpleasant. The food was wonderful, though! A special note here, when flying as a courier, you are treated as every other coach class passenger. If you have special dietary requirements as I do, you simply call the airline two days before your flight and let them know. One of the things that makes Singapore Airlines so special is that you are given a choice of Western, Asian or Indian cuisine, even if you request vegetarian. Your meals are served with cloth napkins and real silver utensils. The flight attendants wear the beautiful national attire of Singapore, an attractive long cheongsam, slit up the side. Courtesy is remarkable on this airline and it is no wonder that Singapore Airlines was rated as number one with international travelers. Singapore Airlines has a relatively new fleet of aircraft with footrests in coach class! No other airline company has made such a concession to the comfort of economy class passengers to date. Until you have flown 17 to 23 hours, you have no idea how important a footrest can be. Just imagine trying to sleep sitting bolt upright with your legs bent at the knees and your feet on the floor!

But I digress - arriving in Singapore; I walked out of the airport into the night air, which seemed to be perfumed with jasmine. It was warm and a little humid but quite pleasant. I met another solo traveler and we decided to team up for the night to save on hotel costs. I'll have more to say on the team-up later in this volume in discussing land costs. Suffice to say that I felt like pinching myself - it all seemed so exotic and unreal at this point. The broad boulevard leaving the airport was modern and well maintained and the jungle was visible from the bus. Exotic flowering trees and shrubs were everywhere and even the night sky was different from any I had seen before. I knew this was to be the beginning of a great adventure, but I had no idea how much my life would change in the years ahead. My appreciation for language, art, architecture and diverse societies multiplied and expanded with each new place visited. Experiencing history and culture far more complex and ancient than my own served to alter my perception of the world forever. I wish with all my heart that young people in America would imitate their counterparts in Europe and Australia who, after completion of the equivalent of high school, pack up and venture out to see the world.

Some Specific Courier Companies

In many cases you do not receive frequent flyer credit while flying as a courier, although this is up to the airline company involved, and as previously mentioned there are exceptions. Flying American Airlines to London and TWA to Rome earned mileage for me when traveling with a New York courier broker with the charming name, Now Voyager.

Now Voyager has a completely different set-up from that previously described and a far wider destination base. The on-board courier can give six weeks or more notice, specifying destination city and duration of stay, or you can go with as little as three hours notice. This was my experience on one occasion in 1995. As I was in New York City at the time, I decided to visit the offices of Now Voyager. I walked from the Chelsea district where I had been shopping to 74 Varick Street, which is located in the Battery near the Brooklyn Tunnel. With some difficulty I found a security door with buzzer and intercom. Identifying myself, I was admitted and proceeded to climb three steep, narrow flights of stairs, although there was an elevator. Once in the office, I saw a chalkboard with various cities and prices on it, and one of the employees handed me a printout of current schedules. Nothing piqued my fancy. The listed flights were out of my projected budget, having already dallied two weeks in New York, or were to places I had already seen. As I turned to leave, Robert asked me if I'd like to go to London for $79 round trip. I said, "yes, of course I'll go!" "Okay," he said, "be at LaGuardia Airport in three hours. From there you will fly to Chicago, and from Chicago to London."

This was more challenging than it sounds. I had been staying at New York Hostelling-International, way uptown on 103rd and Amsterdam. I hadn't packed or checked out, but I digress, I'll tell you more about that trip in my chapter on London.

Later the same year, I lost out on a 30-day trip to Beijing for the same price. With short notice, I did not have sufficient time to get the necessary photos and visa from the Chinese Embassy. From now on, I plan to carry some extra visa-sized photos with me, just in case of such opportunities.

The flights are all on scheduled airlines for nearly everywhere in the world, as Now Voyager acts as a broker for many courier companies. Now Voyager charges an annual fee (currently $50.00), which is payable on the first flight with them. This courier broker has offices in New York, Houston and Miami. You will find specific information to contact them in the back of this book. If you wish to get a preview of their prices, there is a recording you can call *other than Eastern Standard Time office hours,* That number is (212) 431-1616. Stay on the line through the messages regarding use of touch-tone choice and you will hear a list of some available flights. I last called in October, 1993 and heard of round-trip fares to Rio for $540, Buenos Aires, $490, Caracas, $220, Puerto Rico, $225, Hong Kong, $659, Singapore, $489, Sydney $699, and Bangkok, $559. The most exciting fares were $79 round trip to various European ports. These were short notice (next day) flights. I can highly recommend this company based upon my own experience and that of many other travelers I've interviewed. Now Voyager can also help with deeply discounted domestic fares.

On a later 1995 flight out of New York I discovered you can do even better dealing directly with the courier company. I booked a last-minute flight to Rome through Now Voyager for $208, a pretty good deal. They sent me to **Halbart Express**, where I found I could have gotten the same flight for $158, with no annual fee. Halbart has offices in New York, Chicago and Miami, with plans to expand to the west coast. You'll find Halbart and other companies listed in Appendix A at the back of this book. In New York, Chicago, Miami, Houston, San Francisco and Los Angeles you will find listings in the telephone directory under the heading "air courier companies" or you can ask directory assistance. You'll probably find similar listings in major international cities through-out the world.

Most of these companies do not charge an annual fee as their income is derived from those who need their services to ship goods to the destination cities. One example that comes to mind is a film company needing to ship the dailies to the home office for editorial approval; then requiring quick return to the location. Businesses often need to send documents confidentially for signatures and approval. These customers pay a premium for quick, confidential service. The courier company purchases blocks of seats long in advance and can then utilize the cargo space allotted these seats. International law requires a passenger to accompany such cargo on regularly scheduled passenger flights. Aside from the many courier companies operating in the U.S., there are many more worldwide, so you can easily travel on from your destination city. More information on this subject later, in the section entitled, **"Now I'm Here, Now What?"**

FREQUENT FLYER MILEAGE

You can amass an amazing number of miles nowadays through credit card purchases, telephone long distance calls, hotel stays, florists, car rentals and other everyday purchases.

At this writing United, Delta and American all offer a credit card which allows 1 mile per dollar charged to a maximum of 10,000 miles per month and 50,000 per year. I charge everything on this card including groceries, on average $800 - $1500 per month. Of course, I pay the balance in full every month in order to avoid interest charges. On the down side, these cards all carry an annual fee of $25 to $100, so shop around and decide whether the miles are worth the cost. If you do not pay your balance in full on the due date, you need to find the credit card with the lowest rate of interest. Best bet at this time is probably the card issued by Chase National Bank, which allows mileage on your choice of several airlines rather than locking you into one airline; and the annual fee is only $25.

Many long distance companies also award frequent flyer miles. When you sign up you get bonus miles and you can apply the miles on a variety of airlines. You'll want to shop around for the program that best suits your needs.

All of the major airlines have frequent flyer programs and most of these have "partners" - hotels, car rental agencies and other travel related businesses that help you amass free air miles.

For information on these programs, call 1-800-555-1212 for the toll-free number of the frequent flyer program of each individual airline.

Promotional Flights and Cruises

On one memorable occasion I flew round trip from Portland, Oregon to Hong Kong for $480.00. I found this gem advertised by a Travel Agency in the Portland *Oregonian* newspaper. Delta Airlines offered this promotional fare to introduce a new route to Hong Kong via Anchorage. Sometimes an airline will offer a promotional flight as an opening salvo in a price war. If you find a good one, jump on it as they will often withdraw the offer unceremoniously with no advance notice. Recently my local newspaper ran a small item about a $589 round trip for *two* to a number of destinations in Europe. This offer was withdrawn on the first day of publication. Even though I called the same day the advertisement appeared, I was told the offer was no longer being made.

Often, the travel section of the Sunday edition of your newspaper will yield some bargains. If you do not live in a major city with an international airport, check out whichever city meeting that requirement is nearest your home.

Be wary of buying tickets issued in another person's name. You will see in these major newspapers, classified advertising under the heading "tickets" but you'll find they also publish a disclaimer under warning that the ticket can be confiscated if you are discovered. Some tickets are transferable; some are not. Check with the airline before you buy. International tickets must be in your name in agreement with the name on your passport. I personally would be nervous about purchasing any ticket issued in a name other than my own without assurance from the airline that it could be reissued or transferred to my name. I believe the penalties can be severe if you present yourself as someone else when traveling a domestic route. You will probably lose your investment and can be stranded away from home, needing to purchase a full-fare ticket home.

On occasion, airline companies offer companion fares wherein a person on the same itinerary can fly for free or half the published coach fare. This is usually during the "off-season" or it is done as a promotion to advertise a new route but sometimes arises in answer to competition. These specials are usually heavily advertised.

"Free Flights"

Beware of "Free" or extremely low-cost flights given away in promotions by car dealers and other merchants. There is a huge catch to these "wonderful" deals. In order to take advantage of the "free" flight, you must book all travel arrangements through a specified travel agency. The agency then requires your stay in extremely overpriced hotels and resorts. Some tour operators also employ advertisements or direct mail urging the unwary to take advantage of similar offers. If they pressure you for an immediate acceptance, pass. Read the fine print before you agree to any such offer, and never, ever pay anything until you know all the details!

Coupon Brokers

Coupon Brokers buy frequent-flyer coupons from travelers who amass them but don't want to use them. The coupon broker keeps a list of those who wish to sell mileage, buying only when they have an actual order. These coupons are then re-sold to the traveling public, netting the broker a tidy profit. The discounts are 50-70% in first or business class and represent quite a savings to those who cannot or do not wish to travel in coach. Using these coupons, you will still pay considerably more for your flight than discounted coach fare, but less than last-minute fare in any class. If you wish to pursue this angle look for coupon brokers advertised in USA Today and other major newspapers under the classified heading "Tickets & Transportation", "Tours & Travel" or "Transportation".

CHARTER AIRLINES

Contrary to what you may have heard, American charter airlines must now meet the same safety standards as scheduled airlines. There are some bargains to be found in this area that will be worthy of consideration only if you are looking for luxury or for tour packages which include hotel accommodations, sightseeing, etc. I have gotten some great deals on trips to Reno, Las Vegas and Hawaii through charters and I understand there are some terrific bargain charters from the East coast to tourist destinations such as the Bahamas. London is famous for good charter deals.

Your travel agent is a good resource for charter flights and you will find advertisements in the travel section of your Sunday newspaper. Generally speaking, you will not get a better bargain by dealing directly with the charter company and you will get better service from your travel agent.

STATUS FARES

Status fares are created for special groups of consumers, such as seniors, children, students, teachers or the bereaved. Bereavement fares are for people to attend funerals of close relatives and in some cases are allowed for those who must travel to be with a close relative who is seriously ill. Policy varies from airline to airline, but you must be prepared to provide proof to be included in any of these categories.

Children/Infant/Student Fares

Infants under two can travel at no charge on domestic airlines, although this may change. Infant safety seats may soon be required on all domestic flights. When that happens, a fare adjustment will be necessary to pay for the seat occupied by the infant. For now, the airlines are required to furnish safety seats only if the adults request them. Southwest Airlines currently offers reduced fares for children who occupy safety seats. As far as I can determine at this time, parents must purchase the cheapest available adult seats on other U.S. airlines. Southwest is also the only airline at this writing that provides a reduced fare for children aged 2 - 11 years old. A child must be accompanied by an adult. There are special promotions where kids fly free with grandparents or parents, but these are only offered sporadically and generally for a limited period of time. On most international flights, infants under two pay 10% of the accompanying adults fare and children 2-11 pay 50-75% of the adult fare. Some of the shuttle routes in the South and the Northeast also discount for children and youths. Air Canada and Canadian International offer standby youth fares within Canada for travelers 12 - 24 years of age. These fares are generally a little below the cheapest economy excursion fare.

International Student Exchange Flights, Inc.

College students can sometimes get relatively good deals through International Student Exchange Flights, Inc., 5010 E. Shea Blvd., Suite A104, Scottsdale, Arizona 85254. ISEF offers the same to teachers. Students and faculty must purchase an International Student Exchange identity card in order to be eligible for these flights and other international discounts. To obtain an identity card, you must submit a recent photo which measures 2" x 2". You need to print, in pencil on the reverse side of the picture, your name as it appears on your passport. You will also need to indicate whether you are a student, teacher or youth.. Students must be at least 12 years old, but there is no upper age limit. Youths who are not students, but are under the age of 26 will not qualify for all of the discounts, but will be covered by travel insurance.

All ISE flights are on scheduled airlines and are calculated on a one-way basis, so that you may have an open return date or you may elect to return from a different place. On the downside, the fares are less than published coach fares, but higher than promotional rates. They are considerably higher than courier flights. I do recommend these for travelers who want flexibility, though, and there are other benefits and discounts worldwide on ground transport, hotels and other things of use to the traveler.

For additional information on student airfares, work and study abroad, you may call Student Information Services at 1-900-230-8000 ext 112. The cost of the call is 95 cents per minute. For specific information on Student Flights, press 11; Eurail passes, press 13; Overseas work, press 21, Overseas study programs, press 22; for Weekly travel bargains, press 44. I will provide further information on working and studying abroad elsewhere in this volume.

It may also be worth the effort to call the various airlines to inquire about student, youth or standby fares. All of the major airlines have toll-free numbers you can get by calling (at no charge) 1-800-555-1212.

Bereavement Fares

Most airlines provide reduced fares for people who must travel to a funeral or to see to a sick relative on short notice and are unable to meet the 7 to 14 day advance booking requirement for the lowest fares. Bereavement fare discounts range from 33% to 50%. Not all lines offer reductions to attend sick relatives but virtually all allow some discount for funerals. Each airline has different qualifications, so if one tells you that the relationship isn't close enough, keep trying until you find one that is. Be prepared to document your emergency. You can save yourself a lot of trouble by letting a travel agent find a flight for you. Moreover, a discount agency well get you an additional discount up to 10% beyond the status fare. One such agency is Travel Avenue (800) 333-3335.

Senior Fares

Most airlines, domestic and international, offer special discounts to seniors. Usually this is for age 62 or older, although the range is from 55 and up, if you shop around. The best deal I could find is offered by British Airways for seniors, aged 60 and up. This is a membership club with $10.00 dues for two years. Members get special senior economy excursion prices at least 10% below the cheapest published fares. A companion, age 50 or more can get the same low fare. A number of airlines offer "coupon books" allowing the traveler anywhere from four round-trips in the United States to a year of travel anywhere the airline goes. These offerings range from about $430.00 to $2,000.00. Continental offers a Freedom Passport that allows a one-way trip each week for a full year within the continental U.S. Stopover cities don't count and a companion can go with you at the same price. Seating is limited and you may reserve no sooner than seven days before domestic travel and 21 days for international travel (you may purchase international flights at very low prices if you have the Freedom Passport.) If you really like to travel, some of these are very good deals. Be sure to comparison shop, though. Some of the fare wars give you better prices than any of the status fares. As previously mentioned, you should book your tickets with a discount agency, because you can get an additional discount over any *published* fare.

As of this writing, America West offers the best senior program, although the routing is limited. United, Northwest and Alaska Airlines also offer some good deals on off-peak travel for seniors.

Bucket Shops

Bucket shops are ticket discounters. Let the buyer beware as some are legitimate and some are not. In London there are two that have been recommended to me, Trailfinders, 46 Earls Court Rd., London W8 and STA (Student Travel Australia) 74 Old Brompton Rd., London W7. You might also want to contact Bridge-the-World Travel Centre, telephone 071 911 0900, fax 071-916-1724 in London. BTW is a full-service travel agency that also handles courier flights.

Hong Kong and Singapore Bucket Shops advertise in the Travel Section of local English-language newspapers.

There are Student Travel Australia offices on the west coast of the U.S., and you will find other ticket discounters in the classified section of major newspapers listed under "Travel & Transportation" or "Tickets".

Getting Bumped

Absolutely the best way to get a free round trip, getting bumped requires luck and/or planning. Airlines often overbook with the assumption that some passengers will not show up. When everyone shows up, the airline will ask some passengers holding tickets to voluntarily give up their seats. In return, a voucher good for a free round-trip ticket is signed over to the volunteer. There are ways to increase the odds that you will get a bump ticket. First, whenever possible, book on a heavy travel day, Sundays or holidays. Instead of the convenience of a straight-through flight, book one with a stopover in a busy airport. This will double your chance to get bumped. When you arrive at the gate, go to the attendant who assigns seating and inform him/her that you are willing to give up your seat if the flight is overbooked. In return for your help, the airline will not only get you on another flight to your destination, they will write the voucher on the spot. Do not leave until it's in your hot little hand. Whenever possible allow an extra day to get where you're going, so that a tight schedule doesn't prevent you from accepting a bump. One experience I had should serve to illustrate how it works. I had a flight on Delta Airlines from Portland, Oregon to New York City, with a stopover in Salt Lake City. I volunteered to be bumped in Salt Lake City, accepting a voucher in return. The voucher was good for a round-trip anywhere in the US, Canada, Mexico or Puerto Rico. The attendant arranged another flight to New York for me at no additional charge. I had to dash to another gate at the opposite end of the terminal to catch a substitute flight to Cincinnati with connection to New York. There was about a two-hour layover in Cincinnati, so I arrived in New York about three hours later than planned. The only other downside I've found to this procedure is that, being a vegetarian, someone else gets my veggie meal and I get stuck with whatever is available on the flight they put me on. One further note, if they can't get you an immediate flight to your destination necessitating a prolonged wait in the terminal, ask for a meal voucher. Generally you'll get a voucher worth about $10 for a meal in any terminal restaurant. If an overnight stay is required, they'll probably put you up in the same local hotel where they have some arrangement for the flight crew.

Ground Transportation, North America

Train and Bus

The various bus companies including Greyhound and Trailways generally have special rates which are well advertised; much the same as the Railroads. You will occasionally find packages that include ground transportation, stopovers and sightseeing along the way. I know that some travelers swear by this leisurely mode of travel, but I'm not one of them. I prefer to tailor stopovers and sightseeing to my personal taste and budget. On occasion I have been forced to travel by bus and train on the west coast in the US and did not find this mode of travel to my liking. Traveling long distance by bus or train makes for uncomfortable, sleepless nights unless you want to pay a steep tariff for a sleeping berth on the train. On an overnight train trip from Oregon to Los Angeles I attempted sleeping in my assigned seat and was repeatedly jostled by passengers going to and from the bar car in various degrees of inebriation. I had drinks sloshed on me and nearly everyone smoked, trailing ashes and burning embers as they bumped from car to car. Needless to say, sleeping on a regularly scheduled bus is difficult even when you are thoroughly exhausted. I understand that charter buses are much more comfortable and clean. I also found, to my distress, that the food on the train was totally inadequate for my needs as a vegetarian and an athlete. Buses also tend to stop at greasy spoons or fast food places.

My worst experience on a bus occurred when I had a call in mid-winter for a courier trip to Singapore. Because of the snow and ice on the road between my home and San Francisco (a distance of approximately 800 miles) I elected to take an overnight bus. All of the buses were delayed because of the weather despite the fact that I had been assured by telephone that there would be no problem. My bus was three hours late. I still might have made it, but my bag went on the express bus and I was diverted to the puddle-jumper. When my bus stopped in Sacramento, I checked the time and saw there was only one chance to make my flight. I scrambled off the bus and bribed an off-duty bus driver to drive me directly to the San Francisco Airport. I made it with 10 minutes to spare, but of course my bag went on to the San Francisco bus depot. I flew across the world with the clothes on my back and my purse! Fortunately things are inexpensive in Asia, as I had to purchase everything I needed for the duration of my stay. Because of the expense and discomfort encountered with these modes of transport, I am much happier with the independence afforded by driving, especially since I have found ways to do it that save lots of money.

Auto Driveaway

In any major city, you will find a number of firms that deal in one-way automobile delivery. These companies contract to deliver vehicles for people who are moving to another city and are flying; sometimes car dealers sell a car to another dealer in a remote city; sometime a car is repossessed and returned to the seller by this method. One time, I wanted to go from Portland, Oregon to the San Francisco Bay area and I was able to pick up a luxury car to deliver to a naval officer in Oakland.

Another time was not so terrific. I picked up a repo in Bakersfield, California that was destined for Alturas, California. Alturas is high in the mountains and far from any city. The car had a defective alternator and every time I stopped, it would not restart.

Finally, I telephoned the company to get authorization to replace the battery (not knowing the alternator was the problem) which resulted in a 4-hour layover in Sacramento. I soon found that I was going to have to drive another eight hours non-stop to Alturas, unless I wanted to get stuck for the night somewhere in between. This was mid-winter and it was snowing in the mountains as I made my way to that remote place and then my lights started to dim. As luck would have it, the car lurched to a dead stop in front of a tiny, rustic hotel, bar and gasoline station (all located in one building). in a "town" about 40 miles from my destination. This was the only sign of civilization for miles! I stayed in the hotel and called the dealership the next day. Happily, they sent a tow truck for the car right after breakfast. They also provided transportation to the bus depot for me

This experience taught me to *never* accept a driveaway car without seeing it first, unless it was a new vehicle. I never had a problem like that again, and you can avoid it the same way. Always look before you leap into a repossessed vehicle!

When you take a driveaway car, you are required to be 18 years old, to show a valid license and leave a deposit of $50.00 or more. You are given one full tank of gas and then must provide any additional fuel you need for the trip. You are expected to deliver in a timely fashion, allowing for overnight stays along the way and a little sightseeing. You will be given a deadline, but these are usually quite reasonable. Be sure to get a telephone number in case of car trouble or accident. The driveaway agencies are usually very good at taking care of you if you need help. This is a great way to get around inside the United States at very little expense.

You can further offset this expense by traveling with one or two others and sharing gas, motel and food expenses. This also can give you a break from the driving chores and you can make very good time this way as well.

If there is a university or community college nearby, you will find there are bulletin boards in the common area where students post notes requesting and offering rides to various destinations. Usually this is done to share driving and expenses. If the student doesn't have a car, he or she will often pay all fuel expense to the destination. I have utilized this method with good success and generally interesting companions along the way.

Most of the trips I have shared in this manner have been uneventful, but I have learned to specify how much luggage is okay, smoking preferences, drive straight through or with stops, and whether pets are to be allowed. Be as specific as possible and it will save you a lot of grief.

Driveaway agencies advertise in local papers and are listed in telephone books. For your convenience, I've listed some of these companies below:

Auto Driveaway, telephone 800 346 2277 or fax 312 341 9100, has offices throughout the United States and Canada. AAA Driveaway can be reached at 800 233 4875. Across America Driveaway is located in Chicago, 219 852 0134 and 310 798 3374 in Los Angeles.

National Auto Transporters has offices in Los Angeles and other locations, LA telephone: 818 988 9000. Look in the local telephone book for US Driveaway, Auto Delivery and Nationwide located in New York state and Dependable Car Inc, of New York, Florida, California, Texas and Pennsylvania.

Part Two

NOW I'M HERE, NOW WHAT?

Getting there is only a beginning. Ground expenses in any country, including the United States will vary widely and you can get around very economically with a little foresight and ingenuity. The next portion of this volume will include suggestions for inexpensive housing, food, sightseeing and ground transportation. Although space does not allow elaboration in every possible city or country, I will provide some detailed information on some places in Asia, Europe and the United States. You can use this as a general guide for your own explorations and whenever possible, I will provide information about other resources.

Budget Housing Worldwide

Youth Hostels

Next to your passport, the most useful travel document you can possess is a membership in *Hostelling-International.* I know you're thinking this is an organization for kids, but wait until you hear of all the benefits for families and people of all ages. Youth Hostel Membership offers an international guarantee of quality, security and value for your money. Membership is valid worldwide, so you don't need to purchase additional memberships wherever you travel. The cost is modest. $10 under 18 years, $20 for adults aged 18 to 54, $25 for family membership and $15 for seniors 54 and over. There is also a life membership available for $250. As a member you are welcome at more that 6,000 hostels in 70 countries, with new hostels opening all the time. When you join you also receive discounts on all kinds of travel-related items such as car rental, restaurants, books, and outdoor equipment.

The American Association of International Hostels has offices in the Banana Bungalow in New York, 250 West 77th Street, New York, NY 10024, phone 212 769 9039 or fax 212 877 5733. This organization consists of independent hostels all over the world. While you needn't be a member to use these lodgings, for a $5 membership fee they'll give you a stamp in their directory which entitles you to discounts off their regular low rates. Call for a directory. You'll also find a number of their member hostels in this book. Independent hostels are often less expensive and less restrictive than Hostelling-International affiliates - that is, they are less likely to prohibit alcohol on the premises or enforce curfews. This does not necessarily mean a lesser standard, and I have found some better and some worse than Hostelling-International.

The housing benefits are truly extraordinary, with the most expensive being about $25; the average European hostel costs more like $10 and Asian hostels, a lot less. American hostels range from $7 to $25 per night. I will give some specific examples for a number of locations later in this book. There are many hostels in the United States and worldwide which are affiliated with neither Hostelling-International or The American Association of International Hostels and many do not require membership. I have included some of these as well. At each establishment, you will find valuable and reliable information and advice about the area you are visiting. You will also have an opportunity to meet people from all over the world in friendly and secure surroundings. You'll find a wide variety of accommodations, ranging from tepees and log cabins to castles, from modern city hotels to rustic farmhouses and refashioned lighthouses.

Most hostels offer dormitories, single rooms, doubles and family rooms, and nearly all have kitchens in which you can prepare your own food. Many hostels also have cafeterias, pubs or restaurants offering everything from very simple, basic fare to ethnic specialties. Some include a meal or meals with the price of a room. Most affiliated American hostels prohibit smoking and the use of alcohol on the premises, but this is not the case in independent hostels or in locations elsewhere in the world.

Hostelling-International currently offers a computerized worldwide booking system, IBN, and it is possible to pre-book accommodations in affiliated hostels for many destinations. You can determine which facilities participate and book your rooms by visiting your local youth hostel or by calling toll-free in the US, 800 444 6111. When you purchase your membership you are given a directory for your country of origin. You may purchase other directories to make a complete set. *Hostelling USA* lists addresses and telephone numbers for all associations, worldwide. Individual hostels are listed with addresses, telephone and fax numbers, as well as general information regarding the facility.

Rucksackers North America's directory lists hostels throughout the U.S., Mexico, Australia, New Zealand, Wales, Scotland and Ireland, including some places where there are no Hostelling USA outlets.

Discount Travel Clubs

Membership clubs provide discounts on hotel rates for various annual fees. These can be useful, but generally have restrictions you need to keep in mind. The discounts can be as much as 65% off the standard rack rate charged by the hotel, but the hotel may have weekend specials that equal the savings without belonging to a club. Most hotels do not honor these memberships when 80% full, even if you have prior reservations. Holidays are often blacked out. Real budget priced hotels seldom are party to these clubs, so what you get are moderate to expensive hotels, usually at 50% off. Having said all that, if you travel a lot and sometimes enjoy staying in nicer places, a travel club membership may be a reasonable option for you.

I think the best overall value is offered by the **National Travel Club.** At $21.97 per year, it's the least expensive club available without requiring a credit card. The National Travel Clubs offers half-price hotels and condos, 25% hotel dining discounts, discounted package tours and cruises, a free subscription to *Travel Holiday* magazine, $50,000 travel insurance, a full service travel agency that guarantees the lowest available airfares, 5-10% rebates on purchases and last minute deals on tours and cruises. Call them toll free at 800 234 4909.

Hostel Alternatives, Worldwide

Monasteries, Ashrams, Universities, YMCA, YWCA and various religious organizations offer interesting and inexpensive alternatives to traditional housing.

Religious Retreats

At one time, I needed to be in Liberty, Missouri when the local college was full. I found room and board with the Benedictine Sisters at Immacolata Manor on the outskirts of town. The Sisters did not ask me to pay for room and board as this would interfere with their tax-exempt status. Upon leaving, however, I donated a sum approximating what I would have paid at a youth hostel for a similar period of time. I must stress that this contribution was entirely voluntary.

Some monasteries and retreats are set-up to receive paying guests and will inform you of charges. You should certainly determine the pricing policies beforehand. You can find these places through area churches and other religious institutions. You will also find some listings at your local library under "monasteries, convents, ashrams, retreats and/or sanctuaries".

I have stayed at many religious establishments, and have found my own religious preference no barrier. I have enjoyed the serenity and peace offered at a Buddhist Monastery, the joyful noise of a Catholic home for young women and the enforced silence of a Trappist Monastery on the island of Lantau off Hong Kong. I recommend them all to you. Do not allow preconceived notions to rob you of a rich cultural experience. There are housing-exchange programs and home-stay programs in most countries as well; and I'll provide some information on each of these.

Colleges and Universities

There are many parts of the world, including the American Midwest, where hostels and YMCAs are few and far between. In such places, one may inquire of colleges and universities for room availability. In the summertime, there are almost always vacancies in the dormitories at prices ranging from $10 per day and up; and some educational institutions offer year-round accommodations.

Check the telephone directory for colleges and universities in the area you plan to visit and call ahead to reserve a room. Get a copy of "Budget Lodging Guide" formerly named, "US and Worldwide Travel Accommodations Guide". This is the most comprehensive listing of academic housing that I have been able to find, and is well worth the $14.95 price. You can order it by sending check, money order or credit card number and expiration date to: B & J Publications, Post Office Box 5486, Fullerton, CA 92635-0486, USA. They have a toll-free number 1 800 525 6633. Your public library is also an invaluable resource for this information, especially when looking for accommodations abroad.

Some of the university stays include meals and others will have low-cost meals available in cafeterias. Recreational and sports facilities, libraries, museums and dramatic and musical theater are also fringe benefits. Laundry room accessibility is very helpful because you can travel with a smaller wardrobe. You will find that many schools have room even during the school year. I have found the same situation in Asia and Europe. Some examples: In Fuzhou, China, I stayed at the teachers college and received private room and board (three meals daily) for about $10 a day.

Howard University in Washington DC has singles from $14 per day; Hartford College for Women in Hartford, Connecticut offers singles from $12; Marion College in Indianapolis, Indiana has singles for $12. In Thunder Bay, Canada, you can stay the night for $13.35 at Lakehead University. Parkville College in Kansas City, Missouri, charges about $10 daily for a dormitory room. In Australia, you can stay at the University of Melbourne for about $15 daily including breakfast! Twenty minutes outside of London, you can stay at Middlesex Polytechnic during school vacations for $15 daily.

If you are planning a trip to France, there are free university passes providing lodging at about $8 per day for anyone over 16. Send a stamped, self-addressed envelope to International Friendship Service, Attention: Penny Walsh, 22994 El Toro Road, El Toro, CA. 92630.

Special Places - United States

PORTLAND, OREGON

Seeing the Sights

One of the most beautiful cities in the United States, Portland offers all the dazzling attractions of a major metropolis along with the serenity and charm of the countryside and the friendliness of small town America. Museums and galleries, great shopping, a large variety of theater, both stage and screen, a fine opera company and a wonderful ballet troupe offer all the opportunity for amusement one could ask.

Skiers and hikers can day trip east to nearby Mt Hood, which is nearly always visible from the city, or bask in the sun on the pristine sand beaches of the Pacific ocean an hour or so to the west. Parenthetically, Timberline Lodge at Mt Hood was the site of the Stephen King movie, "The Shining". Jack Nickolson stalked his terrified family from room to room through the deserted lodge in this scary classic. The St. Helen's volcano and the Columbia River Gorge are also near enough to day trip out of the city.

Within the city, magnificent Forest Park features acres of beautiful gardens, more than 26 miles of running and hiking trails and a world class zoo. While only minutes away from the noise and buzz of the city, Forest Park seems remote from civilization, an island of tranquility.

The renovated and restored waterfront at the confluence of the Willamette and Columbia Rivers is a treat for the senses. Along with upscale and pricey boutiques, townhouses and restaurants, there are weekend markets with great bargains in all sorts of goods and wonderful ethnic food stalls. This nostalgic section of Portland is called Old Town and has been lovingly and painstakingly restored to recall Victorian charm.

Just across West Burnside street near the waterfront is the old Chinese section of the city. A typical Asian gateway welcomes the visitor to an area packed with ethnic restaurants and grocery stores. Dining at Hung Far Low restaurant, 112 NW 4th, has been a tradition for lovers of Chinese food since 1928.

For book lovers, one of the biggest bookstores in the country, Powell's, is located at 10th and West Burnside, downtown. Plan to spend at least a day there because if it's in print, it will be stocked at Powell's. There are sales going on every day with terrific prices and new and used books, calendars, tapes, magazines and more. You can sell or trade your own used books. There is a nice little coffee shop within the periodical section, and no one objects if you browse while you enjoy your coffee and bagel. This is only one example of why Portland has been aptly characterized as "the friendliest city in America".

Getting Around

Getting around Portland is relatively easy. The city is divided into quadrants with east and west separated by the river, and north and south by Burnside Street. The downtown area consists mostly of SW streets with some spill over into the NW. In the older parts of town, street names are alphabetical. Numbered streets transect named streets. The rapid transit "Max" train traverses the city from east to west and the Tri-Met bus system serves most of the Portland metropolitan area.

From the airport, a taxi will set you back about $30 plus 50 cents for each additional passenger. You can get to downtown Portland in about 20 minutes by taxi. Raztranz Downtowner runs three times per hour weekdays, twice daily on weekends and charges about $8 to various hotels and takes about 20 to 40 minutes to get downtown, depending upon the time of day. Check with the driver to see if your destination is covered. Tri-Met #12 bus runs every 15 - 30 minutes 5:30 am to 11:50 p. m. On Sundays, first bus is 7:50 a. m. Pay driver with exact change, 85 cents. Verify amount before you leave the airport, as fares can change at any time. Running time to the downtown mall is about 40 minutes.

The train station and Greyhound Bus Depot are conveniently located in downtown Portland. The old train station was restored and renovated recently and the Greyhound Bus Depot is quite new, clean and attractive. Car rental agencies abound and the yellow pages in the phone book offer a wide choice of the "rent a wreck" variety for around $10 a day. The early morning and evening rush hour drive is challenging, though, and it is advisable to avoid the roads from about 4 p.m. until 6 or so.

Where to Stay- Low Budget

Women can stay at the convenient, clean and safe YWCA at 1110 SW 10th near Jefferson Street for about $18 per night. You can phone ahead to 503 223 6281. There are only two entrances to the building and both are monitored night and day. For a few dollars more, they have double and triple rooms, some with self-contained bathrooms. There is a Safeway supermarket next door for reasonably priced food and necessities.; and while the "kitchen" is only a tiny room with a refrigerator and microwave with very few dishes or utensils, it is possible with a little ingenuity to fix a meal for yourself. The use of the other YWCA facilities is available for an extra fee. Baths and showers are located in the hall as are the coin operated laundry facilities and the pay telephones. The Portland YWCA has an excellent location near the arts center and the main branch of the library and restaurants for all price levels and tastes are nearby. There are buses nearby to take you everywhere you'll want to go. One drawback to this great location is that parking is expensive and hard to come by. My solution was to drop my things off, then drive about 18 blocks away to free parking, then jog back. If you are less athletically inclined, you could always take a bus, or if space is available, you can rent space in the small parking lot for $5 per day. Women will find this a good, secure place to stay with access to a health club for an additional fee.

Other inexpensive places to stay in downtown Portland are all located in the same general area uptown. During the day, the area is very safe and friendly, but you'll need to exercise caution at night as you would in any large city.

At 1022 SW Stark Street, you'll find the newly renovated **Ben Stark Hotel & International Hostel,** telephone 503 274 1223, fax 503 274 1033. Dormitory rates start at $12 per night and private rooms furnished with phones, television and radios range from $25 to $40. There are group rates available upon request. The Stark is within walking distance of Washington Park and downtown Portland, all kinds of shopping, theaters and dining. The staff is extremely friendly and helpful. **The Ritz Hotel,** telephone 503 241 1642 also offers rooms for $18 to $25.00 per night. Most of these places charge $3 to $5 for a key deposit.

Across the river in Southeast Portland at 3031 S.E. Hawthorne, you will find the **AYH Portland International Hostel.** You can book a reservation through the International Booking Network (IBN) 1 800 444 6111 or call Portland direct at 503 236 3380. Located on the #14 Tri-Met bus line, this hostel resembles a large old family dwelling. For $12 per night you get a bunk in a dormitory and access to a large, well-equipped kitchen and pleasant common rooms, vegetable garden and barbecue grill. An "all-you-can-eat" pancake breakfast is offered for a minimal charge. Coffeehouses, resale shops, book stores, ethnic and vegetarian restaurants, "live" music clubs and $1 cinema-pub are all within walking distance. The hostel regularly provides van trips to Mt St. Helens, Mt Hood and the Columbia Gorge as well as other area attractions. The staff is knowledgeable and friendly. The only drawback to staying here is that the hostel closes to give the staff a rest and for cleaning during the day and you must vacate during this closure.

Moderately Priced Housing Alternatives

If you prefer more conventional housing, **The Mallory Hotel** at 729 SW 15th Avenue, telephone 503 223 6311 offers rates starting at $55. Alternatively, a studio at **The Mark Spenser,** located at 409 S.W. 11th will set you back about $62, but includes a home-like atmosphere with a fully equipped kitchen. You can reach them by telephone at 503 224 3293.

Nearly all of the budget chain hotels are located in or near Portland in every section of town. To get the best price on these, look in the chapter entitled "Discount Travel Clubs" or consult a travel agent before you go. Bed and Breakfast Hotels offer a pleasant alternative to the often sterile atmosphere of a hotel, and can also accommodate you at a budget price if you belong to a travel club. You will find additional budget hotel and bed and breakfast listings in the local newspaper, *The Oregonian*, in the classified ads beginning with #203 *Hotels and Motels*.

Where to Eat in Portland

There is no shortage of places to eat in this city, no matter what your taste or budget. All of the usual fast-food places can provide a fast, cheap meal, but there are lots of interesting places with unique style. One of the best on the east side is The Old Wives Tale. This popular multi-ethnic restaurant is located at 1300 East Burnside, just south of the confluence of Burnside and Sandy Boulevard. This place isn't particularly cheap, but it's definitely worth paying a little more than the tariff at a fast food restaurant. The moderately priced menu offers a fabulous variety of vegetarian and non-vegetarian entrees, imaginatively prepared and presented. When you are through with your satisfying, tasty but healthy meal, you can choose from an array of truly sinful desserts. Great coffees complement the memorable food.

If you crave Italian, be sure to try Lotsa Pasta at 16 NW Broadway. This is an authentic trattoria featuring chicken, seafood, Vegetarian and pasta specialities at moderate prices.

There is a food court in the theater district downtown on Broadway, offering a wide variety of inexpensive ethnic foods. This is terrific place to get a quick bite while shopping or taking in a movie or play. If you are traveling with others, it's a good choice when you can't agree on one cuisine. Most of the shopping malls have food courts with cheap, fast ethnic foods.

Coffeehouses are popular with Portlanders and my personal favorite among the many is the quirky Rimsky-Korsacoffee House at 707 SE 12th. This is a very comfortable, laid-back place to enjoy a cup of coffee and soak up some atmosphere.

NEW YORK CITY

With a population of 7.3 million and more than 24 million visitors every year, it's a good thing New York has more than 59,000 hotel rooms and 17,000 restaurants. The average daily room rate in 1994 was $144 per night. The average meal cost was reportedly $29.38, including drink, tax and tip. Don't be scared away by those facts, as I often stay in the city for less than $30 per day including meals, accommodations and miscellaneous stuff I can't resist buying.

New York, like Hong Kong, is a city of great contrasts. The bustling metropolis is bisected by 843 acres of Central Park, an island of wooded tranquility. Homeless folk sleep huddled in tattered blankets in the shadow of the magnificent dwellings of the affluent. Incredibly expensive designer boutiques offer glamorous up-to-the-minute fashions; but you will find extraordinary fashion values if you take the time to look for them. The glamour and glitter of Broadway theater co-exists with seedy sex shops, live strip shows and xxx rated movies. I never got an exact count of the seedy sex shops, but however many of these crummy places there might be; they are balanced by the existence of more than 6,000 churches, temples and mosques throughout the five boroughs.

Beyond these obvious contradictions, visiting New York can be a budget-buster or you can do it for under $30 a day. You can get a discounted ticket to a Broadway show for as little as $15, pay $85, or get treated to free theater in Central Park with big-name performers during the summer. In summer of 1995, I saw Patrick Stewart, of Star Trek, fame doing Shakespeare in the park, and another time Pavarotti was giving free concerts. In

June, 1996 Andre Brauer of TV's Homicide series was playing Henry V in the Delacourt Theater in Central Park. New York's a great place for all of the arts and you are apt to see some first-rate spontaneous performances just about everywhere around the city. You can amuse yourself browsing at any of the more than 500 bookstores; 10,000 plus boutiques and stores, 65 botanical gardens, 150 or so major sports arenas. Get a stiff neck gawking at 200 skyscrapers or browsing 150 plus museums or, go back to nature and visit all six renovated zoos.

You can also easily get free tickets to TV shows that film in New York just by showing up a little ahead of time and standing in line.

For more information about what's available when you are there, it's a good idea to drop in to the Visitor Information Center at 2 Columbus Circle at 59th Street and Broadway. The phone's always busy, so it's better to go there in person. You'll find a multilingual staff and all kinds of useful information, maps, transportation information, museum and gallery lists, sights to see, tour information, discount theater tickets and other entertainment.

To summarize, you're either going to love New York or hate it; there doesn't seem to be a middle ground. I personally love the place - the theater, the food, the art and architecture, the shopping, the energy, the excitement, the people, the history, and most of all, the amazing diversity! How did the song go? "New York, New York, it's a helluva town!"

Getting Around

The best way to get into New York from the either JFK or LaGuardia airport is the subway. From JFK, the "Long Term Parking" bus that comes around is a free shuttle to the Howard Beach Subway station. That's the last stop. Buy a token for $1.50 and get a train into Manhattan. Be sure to ask for a free subway map from the attendant. If you're willing to pay a little more, the Carey Bus will take you into town for about $16. Forget taking a cab if you want to save money. I tried that in 1995 and it cost $42 without a tip! I wouldn't have been half so annoyed, but the driver told me it would cost $30. I later found that you can ride in style in an air-conditioned limo with a bar and TV for $30. From LaGuardia, the M60 bus ($1.50) will get you to upper Manhattan around Columbia University and transfer to the M101 to go downtown. Alternatively, take the Q33 bus ($1.50) to the Broadway/Roosevelt Avenue - Jackson Heights subway stop in Queens, then take a train in for another $1.50. The Carey bus will take you into town from the airport for about $11 and a limo can be had for around $30.

You need to bring good walking shoes to the City because that's the best way to get around. There are 6400 miles of streets made for walking in The Big Apple, with 578 miles of waterfront and 578 parks and playgrounds. New York's reputation for horrible traffic is well deserved. Because of this, cabs and buses can be very slow, not to mention expensive. New York has nearly 12,000 taxis whose drivers represent 85 nationalities, speaking a mind-boggling sixty languages. The average taxi fare in Manhattan is $5.25, which must be a short trip.

The City is well served by public transportation, so that you'll rarely wait long for a bus, but it cost $1.50 and takes forever to get where you are going. Just for fun, I walked about thirty blocks along a bus route during rush hour and passed the bus, arriving at my destination and waited another ten minutes for the arrival of the bus. If you are in a hurry, the best way to get anywhere is on the subway. The cost is the same as the bus and the service is terrific, although the rush hour crowds can be daunting. There are three good reasons for walking, however. You will see a lot more, it's great exercise and you'll save lots of money.

New York City Beaches

If you have the time and inclination during your visit, you can romp on a sandy beach without expending a lot of time or money.

Five of the many beaches you can easily reach from Manhattan may be of particular interest as a pleasant diversion from the city.

Brighton Beach can be reached via either the D or Q train. Enormous, boisterous crowds are overflowing with all sorts of people. Muscle-bound Schwartzenegger wannabees share the strand with wheelchair-bound elders from every imaginable ethnic group. This is an unparalleled place for people watching.

You'll find a fantastic mix of great ethnic foods ranging from hamburgers and french fries to borscht, pirogi and bagels, great tasting and relatively cheap.

Manhattan Beach, which is less crowded and commercial than most, can be accessed via the D or Q subway to Brighton. From Brighton, walk about half a mile or take the B1 bus to the beach. Bring picnic foods and beverages, as there isn't much available on site.

Jones Beach is very popular with Manhattanites, so it's usually crowded. Getting there from the city also takes a little more travel and expense. Take the Wautagh LI railroad to Freeport ($9.50 weekends, $14 weekdays). Then take the bus from Freeport to the beach for $3 round trip.

There's a huge Mall with food court and all kinds of entertainment including children's and adult's swimming pools, golf, shuffleboard, table tennis, soccer, softball and a large outdoor theater with top name performers. Incidentally, there is also a nude beach area at the east end of Jones Beach.

You can go to Orchard Beach in the Bronx by bus BX5 or, during the summer you can take the BX12. Alternatively, take the A train to 207th, Inwood, then BX12 to the beach year around. Located in Pelham Bay Park and Wildlife Refuge, this 1.1 mile strand features beautiful surroundings, fascinating wildlife, large noisy crowds and various entertainment including lively Latin music concerts during July.

Last, but hardly least is the famous Coney Island. Take the B, D, F or N Subway to Stillwell Avenue, Coney Island. Recently restored by the US Army Corps of Engineers with 2.3

million cubic yards of sand, there's plenty of beach to romp - beaches crowded shoulder-to-shoulder on any reasonably nice day. Here and there you will find ghostly non-working remnants of some of the rides once featured in one of the world's greatest amusement parks. Coney Island still boasts some of the most amazing rides and attractions in the country and you'll find much to enjoy.

The Neighborhoods

Think of New York as a collection of villages, towns and cities all gathered together into a single entity. Picture Manhattan Island beginning with the Seaport and the Financial District. Just above that is Chinatown in the center, with Tribeca to the west and the Lower East Side to the east. Above that, Little Italy is in the center with SoHo and Canal Street west and East Village east. Above Houston Street (pronounced how-stun) you'll find Chelsea and the Flatiron district with the Garment District to the west and Stuyvesant and Gramercy Park east. The Theater District is next at 42nd Street, just below Midtown, with Hell's Kitchen to the west. Parenthetically, off-Broadway and off-off-Broadway can be just about anywhere, but most of these theaters can be found in lower Manhattan. Central Park begins at 58th Street (Central Park South) and ends at 110th. Above Central Park, look for Harlem central with East Harlem on one side and Morningside Heights on the other. Above that is Washington Heights and Inwood. Should you get the opportunity to explore Washington Heights, you will find a microcosm of New York history. Originally an Irish enclave, Washington Heights was subsequently populated by Puerto Ricans, Blacks, Greeks, Armenians and Jews, resulting in a rich ethnic mix of restaurants and shops where the prices go down as the street numbers go up.

Each of these neighborhoods has a unique feel and character and is well worth exploring. You can learn all about New York's historic neighborhoods on a free tour, sponsored by the Municipal Art Society. Call 212 767 0637.

Noteworthy Neighborhood Museums

Check out the Morris-Jumel Mansion at West 160th Street and Edgecombe. For $3 (seniors and students $1) you can tour the ornate parlor where Aaron Burr was married, see the amazing number of dressing rooms, lovely gardens and a spectacular view of the Harlem River. The Yeshiva University Museum, the oldest Jewish studies center in the United States features some interesting exhibits. What ever else you do, be sure to see The Cloisters in Fort Tryon Park. Donated to the city by John D. Rockefeller, the park is located on Fort Washington Avenue. You can get there on the A train, getting off at 190th, then go to your right to Fort Washington Avenue, or take the #5 bus. The Cloisters was a monastery, pieced together in 1938 from relics of 12th and 13th century Spanish and French monasteries. The Cloisters contains a magnificent collection of Medieval art, priceless books, the famous Unicorn Tapestries and other European treasures. It is well worth the entry fee, which is considered a donation. The suggested amount is $6, adults, $3, seniors and students, and the fee includes entrance to the Metropolitan Museum at Central Park.

A few other places you should try to see: The Guggenheim Museum in SoHo, 575 Broadway at Prince Street; The Lower Eastside Tenement Museum, 97 and 90 Orchard Street near Broome Street; El Museo del Barrio, 1230 Fifth Avenue at 104th Street and right next door, the Museum of the City of New York; The Museum of African Art, 593 Broadway between Houston and Prince in SoHo; the Museum of Television & Radio, $6 adults, $3 children and members, $4, students, call 212 621 6600.

The city has many more wondrous museums and galleries, way too many to list here, but these are particularly representative of the ethnic diversity of the neighborhoods.

Accommodations

New York offers an enormous variety of temporary dwellings. Short-term rentals are available in the colleges and universities as well as in private homes. Your choices are not limited to the pricey upscale hotels or a seedy flophouse in Times Square. If traveling alone, there are numerous hostels in various locations to suit every budget and taste. Some of the inexpensive hotels can be a better option if you are traveling with a companion who can share expenses; and some of these hotels are very special places with unique decor. If you are planning a lengthy New York trip in the future, it might be a good idea to get a copy of the Village Voice, to check out advertisements for short-term, sublets and shared housing. I didn't get a chance to investigate fully, but when last in the city I saw weekly rates of $79 on Staten Island for a room in a private home with full house privileges. This was advertised in the classified section of the Voice. Budget housing options in New York City are listed below in the following categories: University and College Stays, Hotels with a Difference and Hostels.

University and College Stays

Some of New York's many colleges and universities offer visitors dorm space at relatively inexpensive rates.

New York University, 14A Washington Place, NY, NY 10003, is located near the World Trade Center, Greenwich Village, theater district, great shopping and many NYC attractions. NYU has summer housing May 19 through August 10 at weekly rates from $135 per person for singles and $100 per person, doubles. For information, call 212 998 4620.

Fashion Institute of Technology, 210 W. 27th Street, New York, NY 10001, telephone 212 255 0018, has suites available by the month from June ll through July 31. Rates start at about $18 per person double occupancy, or $126 each per week.

Located in the fashion district and within walking distance of many New York attractions, the Institute requires a minimum stay of one week.

Manhattanville College, Purchase Street, Purchase, NY 10577 telephone 914 694 2200 ext. 217. Available from May 23 until August 15, this college is located near all NYC attractions and starts at $15 per night with a linen fee. All college facilities are available.

Other New York possibilities: Long Island University, Brooklyn Campus, 1 University Plaza, Brooklyn, NY 11201, phone 718 403 1046, Teachers College, 525 West 120th Street (Box 312) New York, NY 10027, phone 212 678 3000; and Marymount Manhattan College, 205/15/25/35 East 95th Street, New York, NY 10128, phone 212 517 0630.

Hotels With A Difference:

The **Carlton Arms Hotel** at 160 East 25th Street has to be experienced to be believed. This place is a living art museum. Lobby, stairs, rooms and ceilings all painted by New York's *avant garde* art community. Each room has it's own theme created by the contributing artist. One room has scenes from Paris and the halls and stairwells are alive with art deco mermaids and other bizarre creatures. Don't expect doormen or bell hops as this is a bare bones operation but the decor is fascinating and the staff extremely helpful and friendly. Now, this isn't the cheapest place to stay in the City, but the rates are pretty good if travelling with others. For three people, for instance the rate goes from $68 to $84, depending upon whether you want a private bath and if you qualify for a discount. Students and foreign tourists get a discounted rate. All rooms have a sink, and if your room does not have a private bath, there are individual toilet and shower rooms in the hall for guests to use privately.

Another personal favorite is the **Gershwin Hotel,** at 7 East 27th Street between Broadway and Madison. You can reach them by telephone at 212 545 8000 or by fax, 212 684 5546. The Gershwin seems to be the place to stay for young travelers, artists, writers, musicians and models in New York City. It is a safe, well- located and comfortable place with a friendly, knowledgeable staff. The Gershwin is in the old "flatiron" section of New York, named for the famous narrow triangular Flatiron Building located between West 22nd and West 23rd, one of the first steel-frame skyscrapers. It's within easy walking distance of the Empire State Building, Greenwich Village, Chelsea, the Theater District, Canal Street and SoHo. You'll find restaurants to suit every taste and wallet nearby. The rates start at about $18 in a dorm and $56 for a private room. There are mixed dorms as well as men's and women's, so be sure to state your preference if you have one, when checking in. Each dorm has it's own bathroom, complete with tub and shower. The private rooms have self-contained baths. There's a social lounge/TV room, a restaurant and a bar, a rooftop garden and a tour guide office to help you plan your activities.

The Herald Square Hotel on 31st Street between 5th and Broadway is the second oldest hotel in New York. It once served as headquarters for Life Magazine, to which it owes much of it's considerable charm. Decorated with Life covers dating back to the 1800's, the ambiance is one of nostalgia for a gentler time. It was a surprise to find a budget hotel so enjoyable and so well located. The Empire State Building is in the back yard, Macy's, theaters, Greenwich Village, Chinatown and Little Italy are within walking distance. Rates start at $45 for a single with a shared bathroom in the hall, $60 with private bath. All rooms have color TV and air conditioning and are spotlessly clean. At the top end, a large double room with a double bed and two singles or two double beds is $110. Discounts are available on these low rates. You've got to see this place to believe it. If you're interested in New York history, have a chat with Abraham Puchall. The affable owner will tell you everything you want to know about the hotel and the city. You can contact them at 19 West 31st Street,

New York, NY 10001, telephone 212 279 4017 or 800 727 1888, fax 212 643 9208 or e-mail: Hersquhtl@aol.com

Craving upscale? You can stay at the moderately-priced **Hotel Beacon** on Broadway at 75th near Lincoln Center, Central Park, 5th Avenue shops, museums and all kinds of Manhattan landmarks. The special summer prices are surprisingly affordable, at $95 for a single or double with two double beds in each room and $125 for a suite with two full beds and a sofabed. Every room has a fully equipped kitchen including a free coffee maker and coffee. If you need more coffee, or anything else, just ask housekeeping and they will get it for you in no time flat. The service is extraordinary with every kind of amenity available and an anxious-to-please staff at your beck and call. Discounted parking is available. You can call them at 1 800 572 4969.

Looking for a very special home away from home? Based on a European concept where apartment-sized accommodations are better known as flats, there's nothing quite like the **Flatotel** at 135 West 52nd Street. New York's largest suites, ranging from 750 to 1950 square feet have walk-in closets, fully equipped gourmet kitchens, tasteful European furnishings and every bath is equipped with a Jacuzzi. The studio can comfortably sleep four if you use the sleeper sofa in addition to the queen-size Murphy bed. The largest flat has two bedrooms and two master baths, each with Jacuzzi. There's a 24-hour restaurant, bar, business center and state-of-the-art gym. The hotel provides (at a fee) in-room food service, grocery shopping and delivery, secretarial services, laundry/valet, extra cribs or rollaway beds and continental breakfast in the lobby. Rates range from $250 to $450 per day, by no means the most expensive in the city. Your travel agent may be able to get a discounted rate. Flatotel is conveniently located near Rockefeller Center, Radio City Music Hall, Carnegie Hall and the theater district. Discounted parking is available. Call them at 1-800-Flatotel.

Hostels:

New York International HI/AYH Hostel, 891 Amsterdam Avenue at 103rd street (subway #1,9, B or C) is the largest hostel in the United States. Located in a truly amazing historical building, this hostel provides a spotlessly clean, safe environment for travelers with self-serve kitchen, TV lounge, billiard room, outdoor garden, library, laundry, coffee bar, tour desk, hostel shop and very friendly staff available 24 hours. Entrances are monitored at all times, and the sleeping area has a separate monitor who checks for room key and receipt before admitting anyone. Rates start at $23 in a dorm and $60 for a family room. A full-time cleaning staff does a great job keeping this place neat and tidy. The only real problem with this hostel is the location, a very long walk from Midtown. It's a terrific source for information on New York and environs.

For the some of the lowest rates in New York at $14 per night for a dorm bed, consider the **Sugar Hill International Hostel** and twin property next door, the **Blue Rabbit Hostel,** managed by the well-traveled and knowledgeable Jim Williams. He will regale you with some great stories along with invaluable information on New York and everywhere else on the globe. I learned from Jim, for instance, that these buildings are "brownstones" a term which refers to style of architecture prevalent in New York, not the color or composition of building material. These brownstones seem Victorian, with lots of cornices and fancy trim.

This place isn't the Ritz, but it's clean, comfortable and extremely traveler-friendly and the renovation of these historic structures is an ongoing project. Basic bunkrooms, self-service kitchens, well-stocked library and a surprising, beautiful garden in the back make for an enjoyable stay. Located at 722 St. Nicholas Avenue in Harlem at 146th Street across from the subway station, these hostels are in a lively and friendly neighborhood close to Yankee Stadium, famous jazz bars, Harlem gospel music and scrumptious soul food. The architecture around Harlem is extraordinary, making a walking tour mandatory if only to look at the buildings. You can get there on the D or A train.

The only real disadvantage to staying up in Harlem is the distance you must travel to get to other areas of interest, such as the Village or the Theater district. These places are easy to get to on the train but a very, very long walk, and paying $3 round trip whenever you want to go somewhere can be burdensome. You can call them at 212 491 3892 or, from outside New York, 800 610 2030. You can e-mail Jim at InfoHostel@aol.com.

The Chelsea International Hostel located between 7th and 8th at 251 W. 20th Street is one of New York's numerous hidden bargains. For $18 a night, you get a bunk in a dorm and access to common rooms with TV, phones and well-stocked self-serve kitchen. If you plan an extended stay, be sure to ask for a weekly rate and you'll get a discount.

Beyond the obvious economic considerations, this place is very popular due to their practice of providing unlimited free coffee and tea every day, free beer and pizza on Wednesday nights and free beer on Sunday. The Chelsea is located reassuringly across the street from a police station. There's an A&P grocery on the corner of 8th and 20th and a deli on almost every block nearby as well as Chinese, Italian, and other ethnic restaurants. It's close to the Village and within walking distance of all of New York's many attractions.

The proximity of the garment district, SoHo and Canal Street makes it easy to find some of the best shopping bargains in the United States.

The Banana Bungalow located within the Hotel Belleclaire at 250 West 77th Street, New York, NY 10024, telephone 800 6 Hostel, is another favorite hostel for price, view and terrific, friendly staff. E-mail at BBHostel@Bananabungalow.com or check out their web page at http://www.Bananabungalow.com. The New York Banana Bungalow, with rates ranging from $12 in the winter and $18 during the summer, looks at first glance like a standard hotel, reception desk, lobby and all. Indeed, across the lobby is another reception desk for the Hotel Belleclaire. Each dorm has it's own, self-contained bathroom with tub, shower, toilet and sink. If you want a single-sex dorm, be sure to let them know, as most dorms are mixed.

The incredible view of the Hudson River from the rooftop lounge is one of the very best in the city, especially at sunset, and this is also the setting for almost nightly parties with all-you-want beer for $2 and boom box music. The huge TV lounge offers big screen TV movies and sporting events most nights.

The kitchen is self-serve if you are so inclined, but the resident chef, Carlos is a talented cook who prepares three excellent meals a day at very reasonable prices. This hostel is located in a convenient and safe neighborhood right on Broadway and only three blocks from Central Park. You can walk from here to just about anywhere you'll want to go, but it's on a bus line and the subway is two blocks away. There are many delis and inexpensive restaurants close by, and one of my favorite places to shop in the city, Fowad is at 93rd and Broadway. Fowad features designer samples of men's women's and children's fashions as well as some damaged clothing and accessories. Great bargains, but be prepared to wade through a lot of so-so stuff to find the best.

The Big Apple Hostel at 119 W 45th is my personal favorite hostel in the city. The location in the middle of Time Square, is unbeatable (I spent a memorable New Year's Eve there) and the staff is terrific. Best of all, this place is squeaky clean. The only downside I've witnessed staying here is the smoke in the common room, but maybe that will be fixed by the time you get there. The kitchen is all self-serve and rather small, but you can make do. The cost as of this writing is $20-24 a night and they don't normally accept reservations. You may want to call from the airport to see if they have a bed for you. Call 212 302 2603 and/or check the net to see if their web page is up yet.

There are a number of other hostels in New York and I've listed some of them below with a brief description. Some of these hostels are available only to travelers from outside the United States, and you'll find those listed as "passport hostels". This restriction is adhered to strictly in most places, so if you are a US citizen, don't waste your time trying to get in.

Other New York Hostels

Uptown Hostel 239 Lenox Avenue at 122nd Street, New York, NY 10027, 212 666 0559 Harlem hostel, about $12. I went to this place to check it out but never got a response to knocking on the door, so call first. It's run by a woman named Giselle, who I've been told is very friendly and especially knowledgeable about Harlem Giselle also runs an economical bed and breakfast at 134 West 119th Street that you might want to see.

Jazz on the Park, 36 West 106th @ Central Park West, telephone 212 932 1600, http://www.jazzhostel.com. Breakfast is included in the $27 - 37 per night rate. This place is spotless and has a helpful and friendly staff.

Passport Hostels

The Big Apple Hostel 229 West 45th Street New York, NY 10036, 212 302 2603, fax 212 302 2605. Located in the heart of the Theater District, this hostel provides free linens, free coffee or tea and lockers in all rooms. Dorms are about $20 and private rooms $45. The Big Apple allows Americans to stay, but most patrons are from other lands.

Chelsea Center, 313 West 29th Street, New York, NY 10001, 212 643 0214. Although I couldn't stay here, I did spend some time with Heidi, who runs this homey hostel. The international staff is really charming and helpful and the friendly atmosphere, cozy rooms and garden are reminiscent of a small town. Costs about $18 per night.

International Student Center at 38 West 88th Street is open to all foreign nationals except Canadians. This old brownstone is a no-frills home to backpackers from all over. A real bargain at about $14 a night, call them at 212 787 7706, fax 212 580 9283. Located on subway B or C, get off at 86th street and walk to 88th between Central Park West and Columbus.

International Student Hospice is located at 154 East 33rd Street between Lexington and Third Avenue in the East Village, 212 228 7470. I have no direct knowledge of this hostel, but have been told it's a friendly place and costs about $25 a night.

Eating in New York

You can find just about any kind of food from anywhere in the world in Manhattan - and you can find it at every price range from the most expensive to surprisingly cheap.

There are street vendors everywhere, peddling pizza by the slice, egg and sausage on a roll, enormous warm, fat, soft pretzels, roasted chestnuts, Coney Island hot dogs, Espresso and regular coffee, potato knishes and just about every kind of edible. This is the cheapest way to go, short of cooking your own meals. You can get breakfast in some diners for $1.99 with eggs, home fries, toast and coffee. I found one of these places at 16th and 6th in Chelsea, but there are many others with similar offerings, especially around the Village, Chelsea and SoHo. Beyond obvious ethnic neighborhood eateries, i.e., Chinese food in Chinatown, Soul Food in Harlem, Italian food in Little Italy, you'll find some truly interesting ethnic combinations, like the Chinese-Puerto Rican restaurant I found on 8th in Chelsea.

Another food option is the Union Square Green Market, where farmers truck in fresh produce, breads, cheese and wine, often providing free samples. There is also a variety of prepared foods available for sale, some of it very good and quite cheap. Similarly, you will find at least one street fair going on weekends throughout the city. These fairs often stretch out four or five city blocks, and you'll find all kinds of goods for sale, clothes, small appliances, books and tapes, memorabilia and, of course, food. Generally, you will find some terrific ethnic foods, beer, coffee, lemonade and traditional American comestibles in lots of individual booths. You'll also find some first-rate entertainment from bands and singers as you stroll along. Of course, the streets involved are closed to motor traffic.

You will be stunned by the sheer number of diners, delis and restaurants listed in the telephone directory. Most restaurants in New York post a menu outside, so you can check on the price and type of food available before you go in.

Stuff You Can Do For Free in The Big Apple

l.Free dance performances and concerts at the Winter Garden in the World Financial Center, 212 945 0505.

2. Check out Civil War exhibits and get the definitive answer to the question, "who's buried in Grant's Tomb" 212 666 1640.

3. Tour your favorite museum on free or "pay as you wish" nights.

The Whitney - Fridays, 212 570 3676

The Guggenheim - Fridays 212 423 3500

Museum of American Folk Art, 212 977 7170, and the Steuben Gallery, 212 752 1441, are both always free.   Cooper-Hewitt Museum of Design, Tuesdays, 212 860 6868

4. Free exhibitions, main branch library, call 212 869 8084.

5. Free concerts, outdoor movies and special events at Bryant Park, next door to the library, 212 983 4142.

6. Call in advance to attend tapings of David Letterman, 212 975 5853, Geraldo 212 265 8520, Live with Regis an Kathie Lee 212 456 3054, Ricki Lake 212 889 6767 ext 758 and Sally Jessy Raphael 212 582 1722.

Naturally, given the volatile nature of TV, some of these shows may be passe by the time you get this book, but the telephone numbers should still be helpful in finding TV-type entertainment.

7. Watch millions of dollars change hands at the New York Stock Exchange 212 656 5167.

8. See the world's largest Gothic cathedral, St. John the Divine, near Columbia University 212 316 7540, and explore the Biblical Garden and the Children's Sculpture Garden.

9. Take the free Grand Tour of midtown on Fridays at 12:30 pm, 212 986 9317.

10. Discover Art Deco masterpieces on a self-guided tour of Rockefeller Center. While there, pick up free maps in the main lobby of 30 Rockefeller Center, 212 698 2950. You can also enjoy the summer gardens or ice skate in winter (skate rentals available).

These are by no means the only free things you can do in the City, but are representative of the variety available.

CALIFORNIA CITIES

SAN FRANCISCO

The beautiful city by the bay is a lovely, interesting place to visit. The cable cars survived modernization and you can't say you have been to San Francisco until you've had a ride on one. Chinatown bustles with enigmatic signs and mysterious little shops selling exotic goods. The wharf offers considerable amusement as well as some very pricey restaurants and shops. The central area is a mix of shattered inner city and world-famous department stores. Magnificent homes on surrounding hills overlook the city and the characteristic side by side townhouses that shoulder one another up and down the hills of San Francisco. The old Mission district houses some lovely old churches, historic buildings and excellent Hispanic restaurants but has degenerated in recent years. The Tenderloin district around Post and Geary Streets is very dicey at night but kind of interesting during the day. It's mostly a haven for XXX movies and theaters advertising "live sex acts on stage" but there are some interesting thrift shops and some good little restaurants.

Originally settled by Spanish missionaries, the city was eventually populated by the forty-niners, as rumors about streets of gold reached the East Coast. That resulted in waves of folks looking for gold. The great seaport invited shipping interests, and as the railroads stretched west, immigrants were brought in as cheap labor. Like New York, San Francisco is part of America's original melting pot, and each ethnic group, notably the Spanish, Chinese, Irish and Italian, have contributed marvelous cuisine, customs and goods from the whole world. Celebrating diversity, each group harmoniously added to the whole while maintaining special cultural identity.

GETTING AROUND

The San Francisco International Airport (SFO) is located 14 miles south of the city. A cab will take you into town in around 20 minutes (except during morning rush hour) for about $30 flat rate and you can share with up to five others so this can be quite economical. There are a number of shuttles available for hire for about $11 into town. You can call Super Shuttle at 800 258 3826 for current information. SamTrans bus #7B or 7F goes in every 30 minutes and costs about $1.50 (check on the current fare before you leave the terminal, as you must have the correct fare). There's a transportation desk inside the terminal to assist you. Getting around the city is easy, lots of transportation options including my favorite, your feet. Taxis are less expensive than in some large cities, but that could change, so check first. San Francisco is another of those places where you can do nicely on $30 a day or less, or you can spend a fortune.

Places to Stay - Budget

Hostels

Hostelling International - San Francisco. There are two affiliated hostels in San Francisco proper, one at Union Square, 312 Mason Street, phone 415 788 5604, the other is located at Fort Mason, Building 240, phone 415 771 3645. The cost will be about $13-$16 per night in either place. **Fort Mason** is located in the Golden Gate Recreational area, a national park right on the bay. It's within walking distance of Chinatown, Fisherman's Wharf, Ghirardelli Square, museums, galleries and theaters. The **Union Square** hostel (formerly the Hotel Virginia) is central in the city, a great place for people-watching and you can take a cable car at Market Street to the Wharf and a spectacular view of the bay. Both are very large, standard hostels with all the usual amenities. Parking is at a premium in both places. You can reserve space with the IBN (International Booking Network) number, 1 800 444 6111.

Grand Central Hostel at 1412 Market Street, San Francisco, CA 94102, phone 415 703 9988 is an unaffiliated hostel that you may want to try. It features dorms, doubles, private rooms, smoking and non-smoking rooms and provides a continental breakfast. There is a city bus stop at the front door, so it would be easy to go from there to any of San Francisco's many attractions.

There are other non-affiliated hostels in San Francisco. I'm reporting on these from second-hand information in the interest of giving you as many choices as possible. I don't have data beyond the bare-bones essentials but you may want to check them out so I have listed them below:

·European Guest House/San Francisco International Student Center - 761 Minna Street between 8th and 9th, San Francisco, CA 92101, phone 415 861 6634, fax 861 0675. The have a second hostel at 1188 Folsom Street, between 7th and 8th.

•Globetrotter's Inn - 225 Ellis Street, San Francisco, CA 94102, telephone 415 346 5786.

•Green Tortoise Backpackers Hostel, 494 Broadway, San Francisco, CA 94102, telephone 415 834 9060

•Interclub Globe Hostel 10 Hallum Place, San Francisco, CA 94103, phone 415 431 0540.

•International Guest House, 2926 23rd Street, San Francisco, CA 94110, phone 415 641 1411.

•Pacific Tradewinds Guest House 680 Sacramento Street, San Francisco, CA 94111, telephone 415 433 7970.

If you want to get out of the city but remain close by, I recommend the HI hostel at Sausalito, the **Golden Gate Hostel** at Fort Barry, Building 941. This might be a practical alternative if you have a car, as there is parking available. Sausalito is a beautiful little community with a gorgeous view of the bay and the city and great little shops and delis, but nothing is cheap there except the hostel.

Another near-but-not-in-the-city hostel is the Lighthouse at **Point Montara,** 25 miles south of San Francisco on Highway 1. Located on the rugged California coast on a surprisingly deserted beach, Montara was established in 1875. It's a great place for whale watching, tide pool exploration, hiking, jogging, surfing and horseback riding. The cost is only about $9 per night and reservations are suggested. Call the IBN number above, or call them direct at 415 728 7177.

Another 25 miles south on the same highway will take you to **Santa Cruz** and a unique hostel housed in an 1860 Victorian.

Santa Cruz is a super laid-back beach community, complete with tacky boardwalk, great beaches with zillions of beautiful young men and women, terrific surfing and all the usual beach activities. The cost is about $14 and reservations essential in the summer. Call 408 423 8304.

Universities and Colleges

Just north of San Francisco, The University of California at Berkeley provides summer housing for about $36 a day and makes all campus facilities available for your use including the gym, swimming pool, library, botanical gardens, concerts and more. Inexpensive transportation is plentiful. Call 510 642 4444 or fax 510 642 4888.

California State University at Hayward is a little closer to the city and the cost is about $25 a day (a little more with meals). Housing is available year-round and includes use of campus facilities. Call 510 582 4747.

Moderate Cost Accommodations

All of the usual budget chains have housing in or around San Francisco, but beware, they will cost more here than in other cities. Motel 6 in Oakland is relatively inexpensive. You will find that motels located at a distance from the city are the least expensive, but you will have to pay a toll to cross into San Francisco from just about anywhere else. The hotels listed in my discount travel club half-price directories and quite expensive even with the discount, with prices ranging from $48 upwards for a single.

Los Angeles

I must admit up front that I'm not a fan of the city of LA, or of Hollywood. There are some lovely neighborhoods and some of the beaches are great, but this isn't one of my favorite places. If you are gaga about Hollywood and like the idea of hanging out in hopes of seeing a movie star, then this is the place to be. Get a copy of Daily Variety, the showbiz paper or movie and celebrity magazines, and read about where the stars have been spotted and then make your plans to go to these places. It won't be inexpensive to indulge such a whim, as these restaurants can be wildly expensive, but you can always order a soda or coffee. Keep your eyes open and I promise you'll see lots of interesting sights - once I was walking down Wilshire Boulevard and spotted a trio of the most beautiful women I'd ever seen, approaching from across the street. It was not until they were directly in front of me that I noticed, upon closer examination, that they were not women at all. Now, I don't object to other women being better looking that me, but I draw the line when men are prettier! Los Angeles is noted for a number a tourist attractions, Disneyland and Knotts Berry Farm, movie and TV shows among them, but I won't go into those much here as lots is written on that subject elsewhere. Again, I commend those who are interested to various showbiz publications to find out how to visit the studios and TV shows.

Getting Around

If arriving at Los Angeles International Airport, you'll find a "Ground Transport" booth outside each terminal. They will provide up-to-date schedules and price information. The prices I list below reflect the last time I flew in to LA in 1990, so they will likely be a little lower than you'll find. Taxi to downtown LA takes about 35 minutes and costs $26.50, exclusive of tip. Cab to Anaheim (Disneyland) $85, Century City, $26.

SuperShuttle operates here, too. You can call them at 800 258 3826 for current fares ranging from ($9 to $30) and schedules. In order to get this information, you will need to know the zip code of your destination.

Public buses board just outside the airport, and free airport shuttle bus "C" will get you to the city bus center. The fare was

$1.50, may be more now. Check at the information booth so that you will have exact change ready.

Note: Some hostels also provide free or low-cost shuttles from the airport. You will find this information in the accommodation listings below.

The public bus system is well developed and you can get just about anywhere inexpensively. If you plan an extended stay and getting around a lot, however, you should rent a car. If you rent at the airport, it will cost more, as your choices are broader in town, and there are lots of "rent-a-wreck" shops providing vehicles for as little as $10 per day. Los Angeles is so geographically enormous you could spend a fortune and all your time getting around. Walking in the city is impractical and risky, not to mention the famous LA smog which makes outdoor exercise rather unhealthy. In fairness, this stuff is only a problem in the urban locations. The ocean breezes keep the air clean at the beach.

Driving in LA is an adventure, to say the least. Think bumper-to-bumper at a very high rate of speed. You must know your exit way ahead of time, or you may be caught on the freeway an extra 20 miles or so. Avoid driving in the morning from about 6:30 until 10:00 and avoid the evening rush from 4:00 until 7:00.

Budget Accommodations

Hostels

Fullerton Hacienda HI Hostel, 1700 North Harbor Blvd., Fullerton, California, telephone 714 738 3721, Fax 714 738 0925. Located only five miles from Disneyland, this Spanish-style hacienda is a good jump-off place for tours to many Southern California attractions including Universal Studios, Knott's Berry Farm and Tijuana, Mexico. You can take the "Golden Star" or "Airway" shuttle from the airport to the hostel's front door for about $15. The cost is about $14 and the staff knowledgeable and friendly.

Los Angeles - HI International, 3601 South Gaffrey Street #613, (Mail: P.O.Box 5345) San Pedro, California 90733, telephone 310 831 8109, fax 310 831 4635. Reservations are essential from June to August in this relatively small (60-bed) hostel. Located outside Los Angeles in Angels Gate Park, it overlooks Catalina Island and the port of Los Angeles. Walk to the beach and enjoy jogging, walking, tide-pool exploration or whale watching in the off-season. Three transfers on city buses will get you here from LA airport; airport shuttle to bus terminal #8 then take RTD #232 to Avalon Blvd., transfer to #446 south to Angels Gate Park.

Santa Monica - Hostelling International located at 1436 2nd Street, Santa Monica, CA 90401, telephone 310 393 9913, fax 310 393 1769. Santa Monica is a modern, four-story facility two blocks from the beach. This hostel houses the old Rapp Saloon, circa 1875, lovingly restored to the style of the period, now serving as a common room. To get here from the airport, take shuttle bus "C" to the city bus terminal, take Santa Monica municipal bus #3 (blue bus) to 4th and Broadway, walk 2 blocks west to 2nd, turn right, walk 1/2 block. Reservations are always advisable.

There are a number of non-affiliated hostels at Venice Beach, five miles from Los Angeles, and I have listed those I was able to contact by phone below:

Jim's At the Beach features six-bed dorms with wood bunks and regular mattresses. Linens are supplied and cooking facilities are available. The Golden Star Shuttle will get you there from the airport. Prices range from $13-15, $90 a week or $320 per month. Jim's is located at 17 Brooks Avenue, Venice Beach CA 90291, Telephone 310 399 4018, Fax 310 399 4217. Incidentally, Jim is Jim de Cordova, who compiled "Jim's Backpacker's Bible", a guide to cheap hostels and hotels in the US and Canada that you will find referenced in appendix B at the back of this book. Get a copy while you're there.

Hostel California at 2221 Lincoln Blvd. in Venice Beach can be reached by phone at 310 305 0250 or fax 310 305 8590. Featuring shared accommodations for $12 and private rooms for $32, this unaffiliated hostel is recommended by Let's Go USA. Full kitchen and laundry facilities, free safety deposit boxes and lockers, free parking, rental bicycles, barbecue parties and breakfast and dinner service are available and linens are provided without extra charge.

Share-Tel Apartments, 20 Brooks Avenue, Venice Beach, CA 90291, Telephone 310 392 0325. Bunk in an eight-person dorm for $15, a smaller dorm for $18 or in a double for $20 per person.

Some Special American Hostels

Hawaii

Now for some specific and really fantastic bargains! If you have ever visited Hawaii, you know how expensive it is to stay, even in the seediest places. They say it's because the cost of land is very high; and perhaps this is true. However, there are two nice HI hostels in Honolulu which charge $10 and $13 per night respectively. **The Hale Aloha HI Hostel** is located in Waikiki, the tourist and entertainment center only a two-minute walk from the beach at 2417 Prince Edward Street in Honolulu, telephone 808 926 8313. The other, **Honolulu International**, 2323-A, Seaview Avenue, telephone 808 946 059, is a home-like hostel in a quiet residential area near the University of Hawaii at Manoa.

There are two colleges on Oahu which permit visitors to stay in the dorms from May to August, but it's not exactly cheap. **Chaminade University** (808) 735 4760, charges $60 per day for singles and $85 for doubles. **The University of Hawaii at**

Manoa, telephone (808) 948 8177, is a little less for singles at $37.70, but doubles are $88.40.

There are non-affiliated hostels scattered throughout the Hawaiian Islands, and here's some basic information about them:

In Hilo, try **Arnott's Lodge**, 98 Apapane Road, HI 96720, 800 953 7773 in Hawaii, 800 360 8752 from mainland US, or 808 969 7097 elsewhere. The fax number is 808 961 9638.

In Honolulu, you can try the **Polynesian Hostel** at 725 9th Avenue 96816, telephone 808 922 7492.

In Kauai, check out the **Kauai International Hostel** at 4532 Lehua Street, Kapaa, HI 96746, phone 800 858 2295 only when on the island, 808 823 6142 from anywhere else. Dorm costs about $16 and private rooms $40. Phenomenally beautiful surroundings and friendly, laid back staff will make this a great place to stay.

In Kailua-Kona, **Patey's Place**, dorm about $16, single $40, 75-195 Ala Ona Ona, P.O. Box 3547 zip 96740, phone 808 326 7018 (they'll pick you up at the airport, free of charge and offer lot's of other freebies, too);

Waikiki, **Polynesian Hostel Beach Club** 134 Kapahulu Ave., Sundeck 1005, 96815, call 808 949 3382.

Wailuku, **Maui Northshore Inn** 2080 Vineyard Street zip 96793, telephone 808 242 8999. The Maui Northshore is a motel as well as a hostel, so you can choose from singles at about $33 and dorm $15. There are discounts available for longer stays, so it pays to negotiate. They will pick you up from the airport if you telephone. If you plan to visit any of these islands, check the local phone directory under the heading, "hostels". Your local library may have these directories and if so, you can check it out before you go.

One of the highest expenses in Hawaii is food, but you can save a lot by preparing your own and dining on local fruits and products. Even grocery items are relatively expensive due to the cost of importing; and most everything in Hawaii is imported.

I've found that once there, Hawaii is not an expensive place for me, because the entertainment I choose is free, walking, exploring, swimming, etc. It can be horrific on the budget if you sign up for all the tours and other touristy stuff.

Oregon

A personal favorite is the **Bandon Youth Hostel**, located in the Oldtown section of Bandon, Oregon, located on the scenic Oregon seacoast. For $10 a night, one can stay in a rustic appearing dormitory with wooden bunks. For a higher cost, there are family accommodations. There is a well-equipped kitchen and a pleasant common area warmed by a wood stove. When you crave a little self-indulgence, there is an excellent restaurant, called the Bistro, downstairs. The Bistro offers reasonably priced, deliciously prepared meals, including some vegetarian choices. From the hostel, you can easily walk to some of the most beautiful beaches in the world. Call them direct at 541 347 9632, fax 541 347 9533, or book through HI's central number, 800 444 6111.

Continuing north on the Oregon coast, you'll find a new property, **Seaside International.** The location is awesome. Gorgeous beaches, hiking trails and cliffs and the scene of this lovely hostel. Small dorms, outdoor decks with river view and on-site espresso bar are just some of the features of this comfortable place. It's only four blocks from the ocean. The cost is about $12-14 per night. Call HI's central booking number or contact them direct at 503 738 7911, fax 503 7170163.

For more on Oregon, check out the chapter on Portland.

Washington State

Another interesting hostel on the West coast is in Washington state near Seattle. You can stay at the hostel in Seattle when you want to be in the thick of things; but when you want a little tranquility, take the ferry to **Vashon Island.** You can stay in a log cabin, a tepee or sleep out in your sleeping bag if you prefer. You can also rent a bicycle to get around the island. I believe the current cost is $2 for camping out and $9 for a tepee or cabin bunk. Children under three pay nothing and over three pay half. This place was lovingly constructed by the owner and her family from hand-hewn Douglas Fir logs grown on the island.

Property owner Judy Mulhair, a flight attendant for United Airlines, manages the place with a little help from her mother and two grown daughters. Judy is one of the friendliest and most helpful hostel managers I've met. She'll regale you with some great stories about the people who have stayed on the island. She told me the youngest visitor to the hostel was five days old and slept in a covered wagon with her parents. The oldest was 92! So much for the tag "youth" hostels! Judy told me the most unusual visitors were a European Duke and Duchess, from which you can see you are likely to meet some interesting people in hostels.

Nevada

If you like to gamble with the high rollers but don't want to spend much for your accommodations, you will find hostels in Carson City (near Reno) and Las Vegas, Nevada. Two places to stay in Las Vegas are the **Independent Hostel**, 1206 Las Vegas Blvd., telephone 702 385 9955, and the HI affiliated **Las Vegas International**, 1237 South Las Vegas Blvd, telephone 702 382 8119. Most of the Las Vegas hotels also offer very attractive packages as they make most of their money in the casinos rather than from hotel room revenue.

There are many hostels to choose from that are located in national parks, major cities and rural backwater areas, at the seashore and in the mountains. Skiing right up to your cabin or bunkhouse, surfing, sailing or touring the Big Apple - all can be yours on the tightest budget. From Alaska or Canada to Mexico, from California to Florida, you will find a pleasant and inexpensive place to stay in North America with a Youth Hostel Membership. Look in the local telephone directory under the heading "Hostels" for communities not mentioned in this book.

Some European Hostels

Scotland

In Scotland, there are a number of historic castles that have been converted to hostels as well as country houses, cottages and more modern facilities. Most cost $10 or less per night. There are more than eighty affiliated hostels in Scotland, from the Highlands to the lochs and Orkney Islands and the Outer and Inner Hebrides. Imagine a stay in the Loch Ness hostel in Glenmoriston, Inverness, where you can hope for a sighting of the famous Loch Ness monster.

There is a larger hostel just north in Inverness that you must visit if in the vicinity. The consensus is that Inverness is one of the best in the country, but you must see it for yourself.

You can get an Explore Scotland pass for about 81 British pounds, giving you 7 days unlimited bus travel on Scottish Citylink Coaches throughout Scotland and the Isle of Skye, and six overnight vouchers for use at any Scottish Youth Hostel. You'll also get a SYHA handbook listing all hostels, a map and a pass allowing free entry to many historic monuments and castles, plus savings on goods and services throughout Scotland.

Another option is the Scottish Wayfarer, 8 days for 115 British Pounds or 15 days for 185. This package gives you unlimited travel by rail (2nd class) and sailing on Caledonian MacBrayne's fleet of Ferries, Orkney service and one third off participating bus services. The package also includes vouchers for use at any of Scotland's 80 Youth Hostels, handbook, map and discount card.

You can write for current prices and information on these and other packages and literature as follows: Scottish Youth Hostels Association, 7 Glebe Crescent, Stirling, FK8 2JA, or telephone 0786 51181. Alternatively, get a copy of Hostelling-International's directory of Europe and the Mediterranean for complete listings of HI affiliated Scottish hostels.

Every town and village in Scotland has reminders of a rich history and tradition dating back more than 5,000 years. You can follow the "Castle Trail" northwards, leading to the finest mansions and castles, including the magical Craigievar Castle and ruins of many others. You can explore the islands on the West Coast, mystically named Rhum, Eigg, Muck and Canna. You'll see rugged mountains, deep and mysterious lochs, remote and peaceful beaches, serene islands and ancient burial cairns. The wild and beautiful countryside is peopled by friendly folk who will go out of their way to help you.

Ireland

Ah, Ireland, so green it hurts your eyes - the people are incredibly friendly and hospitable in the land of shamrocks, shillelaghs and leprechauns. This is one of my favorite places on earth. I love to ride the public buses and eavesdrop on conversation. The lyrical Irish brogue renders the most mundane pronouncements musical and poetic. Asking for directions can prove interesting due to the Irish habit of answering a question with another question, i.e. "Q: Where is the Post Office? A: Sure, and why would ye be wantin' the Post Office?". When I rented a car in Ireland, I kept the radio tuned to talk shows (yes, they have them there, too) just to listen to the brogue.

Once, while riding a bus from Dublin to Rosslare, where you can get a ferry to Wales, I observed one of the many high towers I saw in Ireland. Curious about their origin, I inquired of the driver. He explained the towers were all constructed by the Celts to defend the land from the many invaders in Irish history. The only entrance to these towers is fifteen feet above the ground. When friendlies wanted to enter, rope ladders were lowered to permit access. When I remarked that this seemed a good strategy, the driver agreed, adding that it worked well until hostiles discovered that they could shoot burning arrows into the openings, thus incinerating everyone inside. When I asked how old the towers were, the driver opined they were a thousand years old. I found this astonishing and asked specifically about the tower I could see from the bus. The driver replied that he didn't know, "but Paddy will". With that, he pulled the bus off the main road and drove to a lovely little pub about a mile away. After exchanging wordy but enthusiastic greetings, the driver introduced to Paddy, the pub owner, who regaled me with an incredible story about the tower - but that's another book!

An Oige, the Irish Hostelling-International affiliate lists 44 hostels. Another organization called IHH offers more choices and there are numerous non-affiliated hostels and B&B's. The HI-affiliated hostels cost less than $10 per night and offer a number of tours, bicycle rentals and other options. You'll also find an extraordinary number of private hostels and bed and breakfasts at comparable prices.

Dublin

Dublin International Youth Hostel, 69/70 Harcourt Street, Dublin 2, telephone 8301766, fax 8301600, is a large, modern facility with an enormous kitchen for your use, or you may elect to eat in the cafeteria. The cost is 7-9 Irish Punt (a little more generous exchange on the dollar than the British Pound). Trinity College is nearby and should be explored for history, museums, art and architecture.

You can walk to the square where the lovely statue of a mermaid languishes in a pond. Curious about the name and history of this landmark, I inquired of a local and got the following picturesque, if not very informative answer, "sure, and that's the whore in the sewer!" Uttered humorously in a charming brogue, this was not offensive as it might seem in print, but I never did discover the name of that monument.

Another housing option in Dublin is Marlborough Hostel at 81-81 Marlborough Street, telephone 874 76 29 or 874 78 12. Marlborough is located directly behind the O'Connell Street tourist office. Marlborough features large airy rooms and great, comfortable beds. It will cost a little more than Dublin International.

In the same price-range, try Mrs. Bermingham's, 8 Dromard Terrace, telephone 668 3861. Lovely old-fashioned rooms, nice garden and sitting room. Typical Irish hospitality is abundant here.

It's tough being vegetarian in Ireland, but like England, Wales and Scotland, you can always ask for a "salad sandwich" which describes the contents rather well. For you non-vegetarians, I'm told you must go to Leo Burdock's at 2 Werburgh Street near Christ Church Cathedral. Burdock's fish and chips are said to be memorable - even a religious experience. It's all take away food, very good and very cheap. There are lots of cheap fish and chip houses in Ireland, and most are take away. Lunch will probably cost about $2 US. Of course you must wash it down with a pint of Guinness, the rich, dark velvet-smooth brew for which Ireland is justly famous. I've tried it, and can vouch for the fact that it tastes better than the imported stuff of the same name that I've tried at home.

Cork

Cork Hostel in Southwestern Ireland is a smaller, more intimate establishment, although both are extraordinarily friendly and hospitable. Cork Hostel's address is 1-2 Redclyffe, Western Road, Cork, telephone 21 543289. It's quite near a major university, lots of friendly pubs, old castles and jails and other interesting things to experience. Regular shuttles are offered from the hostel to Blarney Castle, and if you go to Cork, you must go to

Blarney Castle. Wear comfortable shoes, because you will be clambering up very rough old stone stairs in the ruins of the castle as you make your way to the top of the battlement where the famous Blarney Stone is lodged. In case you haven't heard, 'tis said that they who kiss the Blarney Stone are touched with the gift of gab. Of course, that's one reason to visit the castle. Once up on the battlement, you lay on your back and, while someone holds your legs to prevent headlong plummeting to the stones below, you plant a kiss on the stone. Aside from the gift of gab, they'll reward you with a certificate attesting to your accomplishment.

While I was in Ireland, I found a wonderful travel bargain in a pass which entitled the bearer to unlimited hostel stays and unlimited use of all public ground transportation facilities for two weeks - all for about $250 US. When you first arrive in Ireland, check with the tourist information office to see if they have a current version. From the US, you can find out before you go by writing the Irish Tourist Board, 345 Park Avenue, 17th Floor, New York, NY 10154 or you can telephone 800 223 6470.

England

London and Environs

The best way to prepare for a trip to London, or anywhere else for that matter, is to read the newspapers from there. London has quite a few daily papers, and most of them provide invaluable information on cheap travel out of London, as well as local sales, restaurant specials, theaters, sports and special events. If you cannot find these papers for sale in your area (or if they are too expensive) go to your local library. If your local library doesn't carry foreign newspapers, try any nearby college or university library.

London is the very best place in the world to shop for cheap transportation to everywhere. Check out the advertisements in Time Out or the Evening Standard or contact Trailfinders, 42-50 Earls Court, W8, telephone 937 5400. Many courier flights are offered to all parts of the world from London, and the prices are absolutely the lowest you'll find anywhere. You'll find many London offices of courier companies listed in the back of this book.

At this point, I just have to tell you about the courier flight to London I mentioned in an earlier chapter. Having left New York City with virtually no notice, dashing to catch a flight to Chicago and connecting there for the flight to London, I went at once to a phone bank to call some friends who live there. I found a credit card phone and, fishing around in my belongings, discovered my credit card was gone. I had about $60 US in cash, which I promptly exchanged, then went back to the telephones. None of my friends were at home, so I left word on their answering machines that I was in the country and would be in touch. After reporting my card missing or stolen, I found the British Hotel Reservation Center at Heathrow, London Underground Terminal 123, free telephone 0800 585 737. From the arrivals gate or customs hall, take the escalator to the underground. You'll see a kiosk with a sign that reads "Hotels, Hostels, Bed & Breakfast". They have an exhaustive listing and will call and reserve for you at no charge. Just specify or ask for price range, and they'll do their best to accommodate you, even calling around to find vacancies and reserving for you. They found lodging for me at the Bolsover Hotel, located at 20-28 Bolsover Street, London W1P 7HJ, Westminster. The Bolsover lets beds in a huge 20-bed dorm for 10 English pounds; or you can stay in a crowded 6 to 8 bed dorm for 12. The price includes VAT and breakfast. The generous breakfast includes eggs and meat, rolls and bread, with all the refills you want of coffee and juice and breads, so it's quite a bargain, if you don't mind crowds. You can telephone them at 0171 636 4316.

Fortunately, I was able to contact my friends to arrange a place to stay, my credit card was replaced with a duplicate the very next day.

Accommodations

There are hundreds hostels, affiliated and independent from which to choose in England and Wales from castles to remote mountain huts, as well as an extraordinary selection of B&Bs. You can contact YHA Limited, Trevellyan House, 8 St. Steven's Hill, St Albans, Hertfordshire, AL1 2DY, England, telephone 1727 855215 or fax 1727 844 126 to request a list of all hostels, affiliated and independent, in the area you intend to visit. Among those listed is the International Students House at 229 Great Portland Street, London WIN 5HD, which offers an outstanding bargain at about 10 pounds per night, including breakfast. You can get there from the airport via Great Portland Street stop on the underground, or you can take the A2 Airbus from Heathrow. The facilities include a restaurant, bar, currency exchange, launderette and fitness center. Telephone them at 0171 631 8300, e-mail: ish@mailbox.ulcc.ac.uk

You could also get a copy of *Hostelling-International's guide to Europe and the Mediterranean* for a complete listing of all the affiliated hostels. There are seven affiliated hostels in London, the least expensive is Hampstead Heath at 4 Wellgarth Road in Golders Green (London NW11). This large, 161 bed hostel costs about $17 a night and is located in an interesting suburb of greater London. You can get there easily on "the tube" or a bus. Call them direct at 171 937 0748 or fax 171 376 0667. I have not listed the unaffiliated hostels, other than the Bolsover as the list changes frequently, but there are plenty to choose from in London. Your best bet is to get a current list from the kiosk at the airport as described above when you arrive.

Personally, I would opt for a bed and breakfast in England, given that the rates are competitive with hostels and you can generally get a considerable discount by paying in advance, staying by the week or in the low season between September and May. Also, the homelike atmosphere provided by some of these places is a definite plus. For an updated list of B&B's, contact Aunties Limited, 56 Coeshill Terrace, Llanelli, Dyfed, Wales SA15 3DA, telephone 0155477 0077. They will find you a B&B in England, Scotland or Wales. Bonus - they cater to vegetarians, who might find eating in Great Britain a bit of a challenge, especially breakfast.

Eating and Shopping in Great Britain

The traditional English breakfast usually includes a variety of meats, (bacon, ham AND sausage) plus kippers and eggs, a tomato slice, coffee and juice and some kind of bread - no potatoes. I guess this is not a big problem for most of you, but it's a vegetarian nightmare. When I first visited London, I got pretty hungry before I discovered "salad sandwiches" which were good, cheap and available everywhere. Indian, Thai and Chinese restaurants also present a haven for vegetarians in London, and there are plenty of them. Of course you must try the foods England is famous for. Fish and Chips, wrapped in waxed paper can be bought at delis, in cafes or from pushcarts. Eaten English-style with malt vinegar, it's a bit greasy, but hot, tasty and cheap. British high tea, usually served at 4 p.m., is the main meal, with many courses including soup, salad, several meats and fish, overcooked and sauced vegetables, and lots of rich desserts. A light supper is generally consumed fairly late in the evening. On a little bridge going over the Thames on Canal Street, there are some excellent ethnic restaurants and cafes offering cheap and tasty meals we can all enjoy. The shopping there is also very good, with lots of outdoor merchants offering their wares in large tents or on the sidewalk. Like street fairs all over the world, you'll find goods here to suit every taste and budget, but let the buyer beware. Copy artists and knockoffs abound, and all is not as it seems. London can be a very expensive place to shop, but you can also find some great bargains.

Morocco

Casablanca, Tangier, Marrakech … the names whispered of intrigue, romance, mystery and adventure. Once called al-Maghreb al-Aqsa, or the 'farthest land of the setting sun;' Morocco is an international crossroads known to locals as Maroc.

Tangier's strategic location in the Strait of Gibraltar at the convergence of the Mediterranean and North Atlantic Seas has invited the attention of the world's conquerors. The imperial cities of Morocco exhibit tangible remains of a fascinating past — Portuguese fortresses, Roman ruins, Berber strongholds, Islamic mosques, Spanish and French architectural influences.

Morocco's diverse terrain ranges from modern urban centers such as Casablanca, to the pristine snow-topped High Atlas Mountains. The arid Western Sahara Desert and the lovely wild seascapes of Assilla and Essaouira on the North Atlantic present a feast for this variety-hungry traveler. Although Hassan II instituted a bicameral parliament in 1997, he remains an absolute monarch as he can dismiss the parliament at will.

Morocco is still populated by descendents of the fierce Berber warriors who resisted invasion by the Phoenicians, Romans, Arabs, French and Spanish. The modern Moroccan sultans have not fully gained their allegiance, and in custom and dress, the tribes have remained unchanged over time. The Berbers are justly famous worldwide for their beautiful hand-woven carpets and wall coverings.

For the first time while traveling, I was able to locate and use Internet Cafes. This enabled me to keep a journal, while emailing home. Hurrah! In the interest of providing you with a snapshot and saving me time, I depart from my normal format to include my Morocco journal as emailed home:

TANGIER – THE JOURNEY BEGINS

I entered Tangier via ferry from Algeciras, Spain, and was immediately engulfed in ubiquitous hordes of guides found every-where in Morocco. These rather demanding and insistent men give rise to the largest tourist complaint in this part of the world. It's easier to be tolerant if you keep the very serious unemploy-ment problem in mind … these men really need to make a living somehow. Anyway, I found that saying firmly (with a smile) La, Sho-khran (Arabic for no, thank you) did the trick most of the time. Other than the many marriage proposals any single female is pelted with (for a green card, I think) my journey was manage-able. I'm using a very curious keyboard, where many letters and symbols are not in the usual place, so must cut this one short.

HELLO AGAIN FROM TANGIER

Well, at last I've found Internet Café with an American style keyboard, so here's an update. This place is everything I expected from books I'd read. Redolent of strange spices, teeming with djalaba-wearing merchants and wannabe guides, the streets are lined with men lounging in outdoor cafes, drinking 'Moroccan Whiskey", a heavily sugared hot tea served in a glass and gar-nished with a handful of fresh mint. Women are rarely seen in non-utilitarian settings, and I was told they are too busy at home or work to lounge about in public places. Women who are seen in such places are assumed to be prostitutes.

I found a hostel for about $2.50 a night – an interesting place run by a fellow named Mohssine Laroussi, who speaks English and about eight other languages fluently. Walked hours in the ancient Medina (old walled city) and explored the Kasbah (citadel). On the second day I left my new, expensive camera in the back of a taxi. Thought that was the end of it, but when I went to the taxi station the next day it had been turned in ... imagine! It was like winning the lottery. I'm told that theft is severely punished in Morocco.

ROUGHING IT IN RABAT

Sorry I've been out of touch, but no Internet access was available until I got to Rabat, so here's what I've been up to. I went by grande taxi ($2,50) to Tetuaun, an old city on the Mediterranean. There was a bazaar being held by the Berber tribes from the Rif mountains and, unable to resist the temptation, I bought a gorgeous carpet, handmade from silk and cashmere wool. I bargained the price down to $350, including shipping. Such a carpet would cost at least $1100 in the states.

My next destination, Chefchaouen, high in the Rif Mountains, was extraordinary in every way. I stayed in a fairly nice hotel for US $4 per day. Bear in mind that most Moroccan hotels (other than 5-star) do not include hot showers in the base cost. If hot water is available at all, there's usually an extra charge of a dollar or two for each use.

Any American considering spending a lot of money to go to a fat farm should consider coming here! You can go nowhere in Chefchaouen without negotiating stairs carved out of rock or traversing steep dirt, cobbled or occasionally paved streets. In searching for edible food, I probably burned four times the calories consumed once food was found. I later determined that the evening meal is never served before seven in the evening, which explains why I couldn't find dinner! I have been subsisting largely on bysar ... soup made from beans (lentils, I think) and olive oil with spices and flat bread on the side. It's quite good. I'm discovering there are many varieties of olives, and olives are included in every meal – as part of the main dish or as an appetizer.

One of the things I like about staying in hostels is that one can enjoy solitude or find companions as desired. In Tangier my companions were mostly Spanish. In Chefchaouen, they were French students on holiday. In Rabat, I teamed with some Germans, a Polish girl and more Spaniards. Luckily, many of these well-traveled young people speak some English. The rest of the time I manage to make myself understood speaking French, with some Spanish mixed in. I'm learning a little Arabic and Berber as I go along.

On the bus (5 hours) from Chefchaouen to Rabat, a Berber girl showed me photos of her wedding. Spectacular! She changed elaborate costumes five or six times in a single day, finishing with what looked like a lovely western-style white wedding dress.

Anyway, here I am in the Capitol of Morocco, Rabat. I love the hostel here. It's a well-run place, clean and friendly. The dorms are grouped around an open-air courtyard with an orange tree in the center. Breakfast, consisting of fresh-baked breads and thick jam, fresh-squeezed orange juice and coffee, is included with the $3.50 per night charge. It's not in the Medina, but you only have to run across the street and there it is. I'm taking the train to Casablanca in a day or so, and I'll try to write from there.

CASABLANCA

Hello again ... Bear with me, I write from a European keyboard again, and it is tres dificile. Nothing is where it should be. Casablanca is a huge disappointment, even though I had been warned. Having seen the movie, I guess I expected this vaguely seedy, romantic and dangerous place. Nothing could be farther from the truth. Other than the fabulous Hassan II Mosque, there's nothing much of interest here. It's just another big, dirty city. I had to see it though, didn't I?

Even so, I am truly having a magical time meeting interesting people from all over the world. Youth hostels are the ultimate in democracy. Speaking of hostels, the Casablanca hostel is beautiful inside, but otherwise unremarkable. The cost is about the same as other hostels and small hotels in Morocco, and includes sort of a continental breakfast. The breakfast isn't much to write home about – one cup of strong coffee and a stale roll. There's actually a television in the beautifully tiled lobby. Of course programming is mostly in Arabic or French and I couldn't make heads or tails of it.

I did happen upon a procession (possibly delivering dowry) going through the streets and joined up with them. There was a brass band of sorts and a flatbed cart being pulled by a couple of beautiful Arabian horses. There were gifts piled on the cart, along with male relatives of the bride or groom. The cart was followed by a horde of celebrating family and friends. This provided the best entertainment I had in Casablanca.

The only Internet Café I've found (so far) in Casablanca is at the Sheraton Hotel, and costs 50 dirham for an hour's use. That's about $5 or 6 dollars – more than I'm paying for a hostel bed! Keeping my budget intact, I probably won't e-mail again until I get to Marrakech.

THE MARRAKECH EXPRESS

Well, here I am in Marrakech. I met two women on the train who were attending a world poverty conference being held here.

When it was learned I had journalist credentials, I was invited to attend. It came with free Internet access, so I thought I'd catch you up. I'm staying in the Hotel Essouira ... a beautiful place in the Medina and, at $4-5 a night, much cheaper than the hotel where the conference is being held.

No visit to Morocco is complete without a sojourn in Marrakech. The Place Djemaa el-Fna in the heart of the Medina is like something out of the Arabian nights. Snake charmers, fortunetellers, storytellers, magicians and merchants of virtually everything compete for your attention. The aroma of barbecued meats, smoky fires, exotic spices, the sound of African drums, Arabic music (you haven't lived until you've heard Arabic rap), American R&B and the babble of shouted French and Arabic assault the senses.

In the center of the square, there are at least a dozen carts selling fresh-squeezed orange juice – a huge glassful for about 15 cents. It's very competitive, the hustlers shouting prices and "special deals". Orange trees grow everywhere in Morocco, as do prickly pears and olives. All of these commodities can be bought at astonishingly low prices. Spices, leather goods, pottery, craft items and carpets sold in the souqs make up some of the best bargains I've seen in my travels. Bargaining is a high art. You must begin at a ridiculously low price and then allow the merchant to persuaded upward movement.

Should you desire a bit of serenity, a visit to the Saadian Tombs will do the job. The Tombs were build in the 1500's and served as the final resting-place for sixty-six of the Saadians, including the patriarch, sultan Ahmed al-Mansour. The interior has been preserved much as it was, possibly because various invaders were superstitious about disturbing the dead. The elegant central mausoleum is one of the finest remaining examples of Moroccan-Andalusian decorative art.

The Nouville (new city) is a world apart from the Medina, which represents old Morocco. Nouville has broad streets lined with palms and large buildings. The street names are all in Arabic with one here and there in French. This makes it difficult to find a way around, but you know me ... I persist.

I was thrilled to find this Internet access, although I don't know if it is here only for the conference or if I will have it after this week. The hotel I'm staying in is really lovely. Everything is out of the Arabian nights, all tile and palm with a courtyard in the center and an open stair leading to floors above. I'm on the third floor. My room has a window opening onto the courtyard. I must leave it open or die from the heat, which doesn't afford much privacy, but oh well.

There is a terrace restaurant at the hotel. It's really lovely in the evening, with a great view of the madness of the souqs below. I might just sleep up there one evening if I can get away with it. The two polish boys I met in Rabat hostel and again in the Casablanca hostel are here in Marrakech at this same hotel. They've told me a great deal of Polish history, especially with regard to WWII, that I was unaware of. There are also many French, a few Germans and Japanese staying here. You'll hear from me again soon ... until then ... The world grows smaller.

THE MARRAKECH CONFERENCE

The fascination of Marrakech continues. I'm meeting some extraordinary people from all over the Middle East and Africa here at the conference. It's amazing to witness the contrasts. This hotel charges $175 to $350 per night in US dollars ... and yet the conference deals with issues of poverty in the region! I obtained a journalist's badge, so am able to amble about at will. I forgot to slather on the sun block yesterday and walked a distance of about 4 miles from the Medina to the conference location and back again. I got burned, of course. I got lost, too, also of course.

Asking directions in Morocco is the same as anywhere in the world. Everyone answers with the greatest of confidence, providing false clues that lead one several miles out of the way ... but I do tend to find my way eventually, and it's a great way to get to know the area. The conference concludes tomorrow, and I'll be heading out to Essouira with some newfound friends and then back to Casablanca.

RETURN TO CASABLANCA

It has been a momentous week ... or something like that. I'm losing track of time. Once again I have one of those odd keyboards where nothing is in the correct position, so bear with me. I left Marrakech with an American and a Turkish woman I met on the train from Casablanca to Marrakech. We rented a Fiat Uno and drove through the desert, where we saw many small ksahs (villages). After a few shopping binges at roadside shops, we arrived in the most wonderful place yet. Essouira is on the Atlantic coast, and is unbelievably lovely. The colors are indescribable, so you'll have to wait for the photos. The history is fascinating, going back to the Phoenicians, with invasions from everywhere over the centuries. Of course there was no Internet access in Essouira, so I couldn't write until now.

The two women and I got by with MY French! Because of this I'm making great progress remembering what I learned of the language so many years ago. There were no signs indicating the whereabouts of the Casablanca airport on the main highway from the coast to Casablanca, so we had to stop and ask. Unfortunately, those we asked did not understand French, Spanish or English, and I had no clue as to Arabic for "airport". The Turkish woman had to catch a flight out that night, so we were in a hurry. The American woman flew out in the morning. I didn't get much sleep, so tonight I will take the midnight train back to Tangier. I hope to do a little more exploration of the coast before returning to Spain. I will probably email again from Tangier, Insha Allah (Arabic for God willing). I hope all is well on the home front.

TOUJOURS TANGIER

I'm in Tangier once again, struggling with the àz$£!§ French/ Arabic keyboard again. This will inevitably lead to typos, but the story should be readable. My journey from Casablanca to Tangier was neither uncomplicated nor comfortable ... in fact this was the first time I've lost it since I've been in Morocco. To begin: The American woman I've been traveling with had to be at the airport early, so we stayed at a nice hotel (a bit above my usual budget) located closer to the airport. We got to bed about midnight and were awakened by loud voices, singing, arguing, laughing, cursing, etc. from 3 am until 5, by which time I could not return to sleep. The concierge later informed me that the bars close at 5 in Casablanca and there were numerous bars and discos across the street.

I thought if I booked a couchette on the midnight train to Tangier (scheduled arrival 7 am) I could sleep the whole way. It was not to be. I went to the train station early ... scoped out the proper queue and established territorial authority. When the train arrived, I inquired to be sure I had the right car for the couchettes, and was assured I did. Once on the train I was told I was on the wrong car and would have to make my way to the other end ... twenty cars away. Bear in mind that at this point I'm carrying a huge backpack and laptop computer, struggling through narrow aisles full of people and the odors from the many toilets I had to pass did nothing for the ambience. At the other end, I was told "non, non, non, couchette ees no ici, madam" and pointed to where

I had just come from. To shorten the story, I made two more round trips before I gave up, sat on the miserable straight backed bench and waited for the arrival of the conductor. He showed up as we reached Rabat, one hour and a half later. I finally was shown the couchette and fell unconscious until nudged when we reached Tangier. Anyway, it should be easy from now on, making day trips from here until I go back to Spain.

TANGIER

Here I am, taking an Internet break in Tangier. Really getting to see the extraordinary place this time. Tangier has the expected quotient of seedy waterfront bars and a notorious side, but it also has a remarkable history that would be a crime to miss. It's a fascinating blend of Europe and Africa, reflecting it's Spanish, French, German, Arabic and Colonial heritage in the architecture and languages. There is a large Jewish cemetery and the remains of a mellah (Jewish quarter) giving some idea of the large Jewish presence in times past.

The jewelry created by these nomadic Jews is nothing short of exquisite, and can be found everywhere in Morocco. It's mostly crafted from silver and semi-precious stones. A common theme is the "Hand of Fatima". Fatima was the daughter of Mohammed and her hand is believed to ward off the evil eye. This representation can be found in paintings, jewelry, carving and all sorts of crafts.

The harbor view from Cite Nouvelle is gorgeous. There are four or five old cannons there, the earliest dated 1530 or so. One is Spanish, one Portuguese, but I'm not sure of the others. Yesterday I wandered aimlessly in the Medina, visiting souqs until I happened upon the ancient Kasbah (the word means fortress) and investigated it's mysteries. These fortresses bear mute testimony to the tumultuous past of the country.

Later, I found a British Pub, dropped in and had a cold beer. It's amazing how good it tasted. Alcohol is easily available in Morocco in the five star western hotels and restaurants. As you know, I studiously avoid such haunts except when I want to use a clean toilet complete with real toilet paper. Ahhh, traveling in Morocco, as in any third world country, one learns to appreciate the small things ... toilet paper, cold beer, a cool breeze, a current newspaper in English.

Today I finally found (after many tries and walking my feet to the nubs) the infamous Cafe Hafa. This has been a hangout for artists and writers, famous and not so famous, for many years. It's rumored that people go there at night to smoke ganja or kif (marijuana) but is rather tame during the daylight hours. It was currently supposed to be a hangout for Paul Bowles, who wrote The Sheltering Sky. Actually, I discovered he's old and infirm, and rarely leaves his home these days. Finding Cafe Hafa was incredibly difficult, given the notoriety of the place. There were no signs anywhere and it was accessible only via an unnamed street (more a trail) winding down to the sea between mysterious villas inhabited by wealthy Europeans and other foreigners (including a villa owned by the heirs of millionaire Malcolm Forbes). The cafe itself isn't much. Rusty chairs and battered wooden tables are strewn on a series of balconies overlooking a magnificent view of the Atlantic Ocean across the Straight of Gibraltar ... Gibraltar is visible to the right, the south coast of Spain to the left, hazy through the mist. It's breathtaking and I will certainly return, if only for the view. Tomorrow or the next day I will probably head out of Tangier. I've heard about some ancient Roman ruins and some lovely little caves and beaches on the North Atlantic.

BACK IN TANGIER

As has been the case all along, the last week has been eventful. I begin with the saga of Don Nelson. As I walked down a crowded street in Tangier, a man's voice out of nowhere cried, "do you speak English?" When I answered in the affirmative, he said "thank God" over and again, and "you've saved my life". He went on to ask, "where's a department store" I didn't know, so he asked, "where can I buy some writing paper?" Again I told him I didn't know, but referred him to Moussine (the guy who runs the hostel in Tangier, speaks all those languages and knows EVERYTHING about Tangier. When I got back to the hostel a couple hours later, Don Nelson was waiting for me ... somehow he got the idea I was the girl of his dreams! He ambushed me, saying how he had looked for a woman who could understand ... I said, " understand what?" He replied, "understand my pain." Not knowing how to reply to this, I asked where he had come from. He said New York, but he "didn't want to talk about it." Later he said the same thing about Ireland and England, saying that women didn't understand him (he got that right!). At one point he grabbed me in a bear hug, and I pulled away saying, "don't do that." He apologized and said he hoped we would be *close* friends. I said something like "I'm leaving Morocco soon" and he was incensed ... as if I had led him on. Geez Louise! Moussine's mom (who only speaks Arabic) and I had a laugh over all of this. She wanted to know if Nelson would be my next husband. I said I would make her a gift of him... a gift she refused, laughing hysterically.

The next day I went to Asillah, about 50 K from Tangier on the North Atlantic. An incredibly beautiful little town, the Medina is all whitewashed with pastel doors and shutters. All the art students in Morocco come to Assilah once a year, and paint colorful murals on the walls of the Medina. The only fly in the ointment is the constant "where are you from?" heard from every male in your vicinity. I understand this is only meant to be friendly, but it really gets tiresome. Unless you can get away quickly, it's followed by questions about marital status. Moroccans cannot understand why a woman wouldn't want to be married (which is regarded as the only fit destiny for a female of any age). I have received on average, three marriage proposals daily since my arrival in Morocco. (I've also received a few other proposals, but that's another story ... suffice to say, I remembered enough French to reply appropriately.

THE PIGEON HAS LANDED

But the journey isn't over. I'm part way home, but it wasn't easy. Here's the update: (first let me say how much I appreciate having a good old American-style keyboard to type on ... almost as much as toilet paper and hot showers) I had a restless last night in Tangier. No alarm clock, so I woke four or five times to check the time. I knew I had to get the ferry for Spain at 7 a.m. - that means being at the port at 6 to clear Moroccan customs and passport control. I hadn't enough dirhams left for a taxi, so, carrying backpack, laptop and carryall stuffed with purchases, I trudged the mile or so to the port. While waiting for the ferry to pull out, it started to rain hard and I thought it remarkable that I made it all the way to the port without getting wet. Anyway, the ferry was late getting underway, so I was a little edgy about making all the necessary connections.

Off the ferry in Alcacieras, Spain, I again hoisted my burden and headed out in search of a bus. Reverting to Spanish, I managed to get directions to the bus stop. Once there, I discovered I hadn't enough Spanish pesetas, so had to find a bank, change money and return to buy a ticket. I was assured the bus went all the way to the airport in Malaga and that I would get there in time. The bus ride was okay ... great scenery of the Costa del Sol, the beautiful Mediterranean coastline ... but my bus driver (almost 3 hours later) alerted me that I needed to get off in Malaga and take a taxi to the Airport. So off the bus, shoulder the burden and find a taxi. Fortunately I had enough pesetas left to pay him (just) and I arrived at Malaga airport with thirty minutes to spare. Checked in the backpack (thank God, after traveling a month, it's really heavy) and boarded the airplane, filled to the brim with wonderful memories of my Moroccan adventure.

SIDEBAR – MOROCCO HOSTELS

Hostels in Morocco are referred to as "Auberges de Jeunesse" and charge between 25 and 45 DH (dirhams) $3 – 5 per night. In many cases this includes continental breakfast. There is usually an extra charge at hostels and small hotels for hot showers if available. Here are the addresses of hostels and hotels I used in Morocco:

Hostels:
Tangier: 8 Rue El Antaki, Av d'Espagne
Rabat: 43 Rue Marassa, Bab El Had
Casablanca: 6 Place Amiral Philibert, Ville Ancienne

Hotels:
Chefchaouen: Pension Znika, 4 Rue Znika, 25/45 DH
                         Hotel Rif, Avenida Hassan II, 50/125 DH
Marrakech:Hotel Essouira, the Medina, 30/75 DH
Essouira:Hotel Smara, Rue de la Skala, 50/90 DH
Assilah:Hotel Mansour 49 Ave Mohammed V, 140/195 DH

A publication I found extremely useful: *Morocco*, published by Lonely Planet Publications. I recommend it to you.

Italy

Some Generalities

From the bustling cities to the lovely coastal villages and countryside, Italy has much to offer the traveler and needn't be too expensive. If you are going to be there for a while, get a Eurail pass before leaving home and you'll experience considerable savings. Your travel agent can arrange it for you as can Hostelling-International. Bus and train service is very good throughout Italy, but watch out for pickpockets. They are extremely clever and seem to operate in pairs or groups. One or more will divert your attention, sometimes bumping into you or creating noise, while another deftly lifts your valuables. This is usually accomplished without your awareness - indeed you won't know your wallet is gone until the next time you need it. You also need to be careful of cameras and bags while walking around as thieves on motorcycles rip them out of your arms while speeding by. Wherever you go, it's best to leave expensive jewelry at home and carry cash, documents and credit cards in the kind of pouch that can be secreted inside your clothing. The hostel shops and AAA offices sell such pouches. I also like a fanny pack, but never wear it with the pouch in back - keep in front where you can see it. Standing in a crowded bus or train or in any other crowd situation, keep one hand on the opening of the pack. Don't hitch, it's considered an invitation for exploitation, sexual or otherwise. Walking around is the best way to save money, avoid pickpockets and crowds and you'll see the most wonderful sights. The water available in fountains is drinkable. They're designed so that if you plug one opening with your finger, water will spout from a different opening. I learned to carry a water bottle around just to take advantage of these fountains. If you need to use a toilet it is perfectly proper to go into any business establishment and ask, "Do vay la toletta". The spelling is only an approximation but that's how to say it. Another phrase I found invaluable, being a vegetarian, was "sono vegetariana". I believe a male would say "vegetariano". Expect nearly everything to close from about 1 p.m. until 3 or 4 p.m., when all sensible Italians retire for a large meal and a rest.

Accommodations

Italy has an amazing network of more than 50 hostels scattered throughout the countryside. Expect to pay 15,000 to 25,000 lire, or about $9 to 15 US dollars, usually including sheets and breakfast. Italian hostels do not typically allow hostlers to cook their own meals, but you can bring in deli-style foods one meal at a time. Most hostels include breakfast in their rates, as do many of the small pensione, but don't expect an American or English-style meal. Italians prefer *petit dejeuner* in the French manner, consisting of a roll or other bread, coffee and juice. Camping is generally the most economic form of accommodation, costing on average, 7,000 lire per person plus another 7000 per car. Convents provide another alternative, costing about the same as hostels, while providing a little more quiet. Some of the convents allow men, some don't. If travelling with others, you might stay in the pensione for about the same as the hostels. The least expensive pensione are about 23,000 lire, and if you go this route, ask to see the room first. For women, the best value in Italy are the Protezione della Giovane, which are dorms provided by religious orders. These generally cost around 14,000 lire and are clean and well-maintained. Most have age restrictions, serving young women only.

Dining in Italy

Eating in Italy can consume a huge part of your budget unless you plan carefully. Keep in mind that there is a hierarchy of eating establishments. I must reluctantly advise that American style fast food places such as MacDonalds, really are relatively cheap. Budget-wise, the open-air market is your best bet for all kinds of delicacies including pizza, wonderful cheese, fresh fruit and bakery goods, beverages, lunchmeats and cooked sausage. Next, try the alimentari, a kind of deli-grocery, which offers sandwiches, cheese, meats, breads and other components of a great picnic meal at a reasonable price. Rosticcerie provide hot take-out meals as do the local groceries and supermarkets. Tavola and bars have foods with three distinct prices, most expensive is sitting at a sidewalk table, and sitting inside the place is a little less. The least expensive option is to eat while standing at the bar inside. Sit-down restaurants usually have a cover charge of about $1.50 - $2.00. The osterie, trattoria and ristoranti are most expensive. I actually found a Chinese ristoranti near the Trevi fountain that was reasonably priced, and upon further exploration confirmed that Chinese food is cheap in Italy when you can find it.

Rome

If you ever get a chance to explore Europe, Rome should be a priority. The art and architecture alone make for a memorable visit. The co-mingling of modern and ancient Rome, the ancient Etruscan gods and Catholicism add to the fascination of the "Eternal City". If you have very limited time and want to start with an oversight, I recommend the Roma Trolley Tour for 26,000 lire. This is good for 24 hours and you can get on and off at all the most fascinating places in Rome. If you do this on the first day, you can more easily plan out the rest of your visit, returning to those places offering the most interest.

You'll be overwhelmed by the multitude of fountains and statuary. Monuments and art both sacred and profane designed by Botticelli, Michelangelo, Raphael and DaVinci are everywhere. You will notice the capital letter "B" and images of bees everywhere. I believe these were the "trademark" of Gian Lorenzo Bernini, a gifted sculptor and painter who died in 1680 at the age of 81. Bernini's works can be found everywhere in Rome; some of the most famous at Villa Borghese. You can see the beginning and end of his career in Rome; beginning at the Church of Santa Bibiana which was Bernini's first architectural commission. Pope Urban VIII commissioned Bernini to remodel the ancient basilica in 1625. Bernini, who was 27 years old at the time, remade the facade and sculpted an extraordinary free-standing statue of the saint. Bernini also created the exquisite oval chapel in the Jesuit seminary of Sant' Andrea al Quirinale, an undertaking which consumed twenty years and was completed in 1678. You'll find two self-portraits of the artist in the painting gallery at San Michele in the Trastevere district.

In Trastevere, the National Gallery of Art, located in the Palazzo Corsini houses many great works of art, including *St. Sebastian* by Rubens, Rest on the *Flight into Egypt* by Van Dyck, *St. John the Baptist* by Caravaggio and *Views of Venice* by Canaletto. Some of the world's most remarkable works of Bernini and many other greats can be viewed in St. Peter's Basilica. Be sure to see the tomb of Pope Alexander VII located over the doorway to the sacristy. This was the last of Bernini's works.

St Peter's Basilica is free to visitors and features Michelangelo's *Pieta*, the statue of the grieving Madonna, cradling the dead body of Christ. St. Peter's Chair by Bernini represents the ornate celebration of faith extant in Rome.

The Piazza del Campidoglio, conceived by Michelangelo, consists of a trapezoid defined by three palaces, the Palazzo dei Conservatori, the Palazzo Nuovo which houses the wonderful Capitoline Museum, and the Palazzo Senatorio. An imposing staircase guarded by lions leads to the piazza and the colossal statues of Castor and Pollux with their horses, flanked by statues of Constantine and Constantine II and impressive columns from the Via Appia. In the center of the Piazza is the spectacular equestrian statue of Marcus Aurelius. This work was cast in bronze in the 2nd century AD and brought to the Piazza by Pope Paul III in 1538 against the wishes of Michelangelo.

The Palazzo Nuovo was designed by Michelangelo but not built until the 17th century. It houses the Capitoline Museum which stores and exhibits some of the world's most remarkable works of ancient art. The 5th century BC statue of Minerva is found in the atrium of the ground floor, near the Egyptian Collection. On the first floor, the Room of the Doves contains the fine mosaic attributed to Sosus of Pergamon and the Tabula Iliaca, a relief of the destruction of Troy. The Cabinet of Venus houses the exquisite Capitoline Venus, recreated in the 2nd century BC from an earlier work. The Room of the Emperors and the Room of the Philosophers contain collections of busts of roman emperors and the great philosophers. Be sure to see the statue at the center of the Room of the Dying Gaul.

The Sistine Chapel in the Vatican Museum alone is worth at least half a day - in fact you could return every day of your stay in Rome and not see everything. Unfortunately, it's not free except on the last Sunday of the month. Apparently that's traditional in Rome, as most museums charge nothing on the last Sunday of the month. Normally the cost is 13,000 lire. To get the most out of your visit, go at 8:45 am, as the museum closes at 1:45 for the afternoon siesta. Before you go to Rome, go to your local library and read up on the Vatican museum, St. Peters Basilica and the Sistine Chapel. That way you'll know what to look for. They sell a very nice souvenir book around Rome entitled, "Rome and Vatican" for about 12,000 lire. It's worth the price because of the foldout pictures of the Sistine Chapel and excellent photos of many other places you'll want to see. The book is published by plurigraf, Narni-Teri, Italia and is sold at kiosks and bookstores in Rome.

When visiting any of the churches of Rome, observe the custom and wear modest clothing to avoid offending at the least; and being denied entrance at the worst. Shoulders should not be bare and shorts or short skirts are generally not allowed.

There are so many wonderful museums in Rome featuring an extraordinary variety of both religious art and ancient artifacts. One of the most bizarre sights in all of Europe is housed in the church of Santa Maria della Concezione, located at Via Vittorio Veneto 27. The church itself is nothing special for Rome, but beneath the nave, built on mud brought from Jerusalem on the orders of Pope Urban VIII, are chambers decorated with the remains of 4000 Capuchin monks. Each chamber has a motif and contains some whole mummified remains as well as pictures made up from human bones. My first reaction was one of revulsion (all I could think of was the story of lampshades made from the skin of the Jews of the concentration camps). More bones make up ornate ceiling decorations, archways and lamps. The last chamber explains the rather macabre art in sympathetic terms. One skeleton represents death with more bones making up a scythe and hourglass. Above all, an angel presides. The representation is of the triumph of faith over death. Photographs are not allowed, most likely to promote sales of numerous post cards and photos in the lobby. A "donation" is required by a monk who stands guard at the entrance.

Getting lost in Rome yields a delightful and unexpected bonus. Alleys circle around and the narrow, cobbled streets hide imposing ancient churches filled with splendid artworks by the old masters. I spent many days just walking around, ogling the remains of the Roman Forum and the Coliseum and the statuary that characterizes the eternal city.

Special Places, Asia
Singapore

The name "Singapore" is a modernization of "Singapura", meaning "Lion City". As the legend goes, Sang Nila Utama, Prince of Palembang visited the island and reported seeing a lion "very swift and beautiful, its body bright red, its head jet black." What he lacked in knowledge of zoology, the prince made up in imagination. The beast he observed was undoubtedly a tiger. Today, even the tigers are confined to the wildlife park, but the name stuck.

From Changi Airport in Singapore, you may taxi into town for about $10, U.S. You will need to change some money in the airport unless you have arranged for some at home. I'll explain how to do that in the section on general travel tips. Don't change a large amount of cash, as you will find a much better rate of exchange from any of the authorized moneychangers in town. Banks charge a larger fee than the moneychangers, as well. Best bet - ask the money -changer how much you will get for $100 US or some other specified amount. Have them write the amount for you. Ask if you can get a more favorable rate with more money. There is also usually a better rate for cash than for travelers' checks.

The most practical alternative is to find someone to share a taxi into Singapore. From Basement #2 of the airport you can take bus #390, which runs every 15 minutes from 6 a.m. to 11:45 p.m. You may have to hustle to make the last bus as many courier flights arrive as late at 10:30 p.m.

Housing in Singapore

'Housing in Singapore is somewhat complicated. You will find the small traditional Chinese hotels most interesting and relatively inexpensive, but be prepared to bargain! In fact, you should be prepared to bargain for almost everything in Singapore. It is expected, and the first price asked is apt to be much higher than you need to pay. I have found that many of the smaller Chinese hotels will run about $20 per night for a double, They usually charge the same for one person as two; I have never encountered a set price for a single. Obviously you can save significantly if you find someone to team up with but choose carefully. A traveler I met in Singapore (Ann) told me of teaming up with another single woman of her age who was also traveling as a courier. From that, Ann assumed they would share a common philosophy. Much to Ann's displeasure and discomfort, the other woman was very timid and paranoid in situations Ann enjoyed exploring. The woman complained about everything and hogged the bathroom. On the other hand, I have met many adventurous and kindred souls who have enhanced my travel enjoyment. Some have become lifelong friends. Spend a little time discussing travel plans and your individual travel style before making a commitment and you will reap dividends.

The South East Asia Hotel at 180 Waterloo and the Bencoolen Hotel at 47 Bencoolen Street are two of my favorite small hotels in Singapore. Each charges about $25 per night if you bargain for it. You will get a better price if you indicate that you are staying longer. I especially liked the South East Asia because of its proximity to a large hawker center (more about these later) and all kinds of shopping. I found I could walk from either of these hotels to many places of interest and if not, there were frequent buses nearby.

The Chinese YMCA, 70 Palmer Road and the YWCA at 8 Fort Canning Road offer simple and inexpensive housing, but I found the locations less convenient than the above-mentioned hotels. There are no youth hostels as of this writing. Because Singapore is a small island with a very large population, both indigent and transient, housing space is at a premium. Most of the Western hotels are quite expensive. Usually when I visit Singapore now, I stay with friends or I cross the causeway to Malaysia, where housing and everything else is very cheap. Still, there are many things to see in Singapore that are worthwhile and there are many fantastic bargains for the alert shopper.

Singapore water is safe and clean. In fact, you will find this one of the cleanest places in the world - much cleaner than many American cities. There are enormous fines for littering, spitting in the street and, for permanent residents, even chewing gum can be illegal! I think they expect and accept a little barbarism from tourists, but you are not allowed to bring more chewing gum into Singapore than you can reasonably consume. There is also a fine for failing to flush a public toilet. There are numerous public toilets, but be sure to carry tissue with you. These toilets are rarely equipped with paper, and the stuff they sell on site is rough and stretchy. It's cheap, though! You may also encounter your first Chinese-style toilet. This is usually a keyhole shaped hole in the floor (flush with the floor if you don't mind the pun) or it may be mounted on a platform. One squats, rather than sits - a more hygienic method, if you think about it.

If you yearn for a more Western facility, just visit any of the Western hotels or restaurants. They have no apparent objections to people coming in to use them. I often stop in just to have the luxury of washing my hands and face with soap and warm water while I'm out and about.

Sightseeing

The National Museum houses some extraordinary exhibits worthy of investigation and The University of Singapore's Art Collection offers a comprehensive look into 4000 years of Chinese porcelain. Ancient Asian fabrics and Indian sculpture are also displayed. The Singapore Zoo rivals any in the world. There are extraordinary beasts and birds, lizards and other fascinating creatures from all over the world. There are interesting exhibits and a first-rate aquarium and you can ride an elephant if you are so inclined. There are some absolutely gorgeous free public beaches to enjoy.

You can also take a boat or a tram to Sentosa Island. I highly recommend it. Take a camera and lots of film because this is a sightseeing paradise. It costs about $7 for admittance to the island and you can stay as long as you want. There is housing here but it is quite expensive. Camping out on the beach is permitted, though, and the weather is nearly always fine for camping. There are pre-erected tents available for rental at cheap rates. Singapore is only one degree from the equator and the year-round temperature is about 85 Fahrenheit with about 80% (or higher) humidity. Do not bring warm clothing to this part of the world.

On Sentosa you will find all sorts of wildlife and there is a train that chugs around continuously which allows unlimited ridership for about $4. You can get on and off wherever you please. I once found a whole tribe of monkeys here and watched while they enjoyed their lunch, played, wrestled and socialized. Be careful not to get too close, though. These primates have sharp teeth and are very territorial, as I discovered. I watched and photographed them for nearly an hour with no problem; but when I turned to leave, the leader noticed me for the first time. He immediately charged, fangs bared. Not knowing how else to react, I faced him and stood very still.

There we stood, all of the monkeys on alert and one worried traveler trying to look resolute and unafraid. After a number of aborted attempts to leave, the monkeys lost interest and I backed away. I must admit that in order to get close to their enclave I had to leave the beaten path, which I probably should not have done. However, I also felt that the experience was worth it.

Sentosa has quite a few attractions, restaurants and shops as well as clean, sunny beaches. You can rent a bicycle, if you like, and explore that way but be sure to wear a sun block and a hat. You really don't want to spend your vacation time in a hospital. One of my favorite places on the island is a museum dedicated to the history of Singapore. The exhibits are well executed and presented in an entertaining manner. In particular, a whole section is dedicated to the defeat and occupation by the Japanese and the subsequent liberation of Singapore during World War II. You will find an exotic 18-hole golf course, a skating rink, an oceanarium and a lovely swimming lagoon on Sentosa.

Eating in Singapore

You can tour the world, gastronomically speaking, in Singapore. I can't thing of any dining tradition that would not be available here. American fast food, Italian pizza & spaghetti, Thai delicacies, Indian curries, French pastries, Russian caviar; anything your appetite requires can be found somewhere on this cosmopolitan island.

There are traditional "restaurants" called Hawker stands. Originally, these were mobile carts that roamed the island offering delicious hot or cold foods and beverages at incredibly low prices. Today, Hawker stands are regulated, inspected and most immobile. They are often located in buildings called hawker centers that look like high-rise parking facilities. In these hawker centers, you will find several floors occupied by hundreds of these small eateries with some very cheap shopping on the other floors. Some are located in the basements of smart, modern shopping malls and some can be found in outdoor markets. These Hawker stands offer Chinese, Malay, Indian, Muslim, Thai, Japanese and many other ethnic foods. A complete meal costs about $2.

You will also find fresh fruit stands offering Jackfruit, Starfruit, Durian, Mangosteen, Lychee, Rambutan, Rock Melon, Mango, Guava and a host of other exotic fruits as well as some more familiar. You can purchase the fresh, juicy fruit impaled on a wooden skewer for your convenience, or you can have it juiced and served as a beverage.

Durian is usually purchased whole and is a story unto itself. When first I saw this curious fruit, I asked a local what it was. The Singaporean laughingly insisted that only natives could eat durian. I took that as a dare, of course, and purchased some to try. Durian can be a small as a grapefruit or as large as a watermelon. It resembles a large melon with spikes. Once cut into, there is an overpowering stench, much like an open sewer. Once past the smell, I found the small pouches of flesh within quite tasty. The smell is so distasteful, hotels in Asia forbid bringing it to your room. Signs are posted sternly warning of eviction if you bring it in.

Hot, strong, oily Chinese coffee is served in these places too, but unless you want cream and sugar, specify plain, black coffee or tea. Chinese coffee is wonderful, strong stuff! Try saying "Teh oh!" when you want tea. Tea, of course, is sold everywhere and comes in every variety available in the world. If you want to discover the British tradition of high tea, you must visit Raffles Hotel. Raffles Hotel is very expensive, but it's a major historic monument in Singapore and should be seen. It is a Singaporean institution, oozing British colonial history. Originally it was a "tiffin" house, colonial era terminology for a curry lunch. Later, it was taken over by some Armenian entrepreneurs who built a string of famous Asian hotels. Raffles Hotel has been mentioned in many fictional works by authors such as Joseph Conrad and Somerset Maugham. Rudyard Kipling recommended the food! The famous Raffles Long Bar served the first Singapore Sling in 1915, and you can sit at the same bar and order one today.

I discovered after several years of visiting that there are Hawker Stands on one of the upper floors at Singapore Changi Airport. Prices there are higher than other stands in town, but still much cheaper (and much tastier) than the usual airport fare available elsewhere in Changi airport or at any other airport in the world, for that matter. There are also many more familiar types of restaurants all over Singapore, offering the best from everywhere along with the usual American Fast Food fare. Even at these places, prices compare favorably with others. If you like Indian food, or just want to try it, I particularly recommend the Bombay Woodlands Restaurant on Orchard Road for some of the best Indian vegetarian food I've ever experienced.

Shopping in Singapore

By all means, go the Orchard Road to see where the tourists shop and pay prices worthy of Rodeo Drive or Saville Row; then go around to the ethnic areas for real bargains. Singapore is divided into ethnic enclaves. Historically, the various races in this part of the world were constantly at war. In order to create an orderly society, the Singaporean government decreed that each group would live in separate areas - de facto segregation. The Chinese attend Chinese schools and live in the Chinese district, and the British, Malaysians, Indians and others do the same. Because of this, you will find Arab Street, which is a sector rather than a street, offering silks, bangles, incense, middle eastern goods and foods. You will find a variety of everyday and exotic wares in the sector, and the aromatic little cafes will tempt you at every turn. There is also an area where you will find whole blocks of shops and showrooms selling fabrics and sewing notions from India, China and Thailand at remarkably low prices. There are, throughout Singapore, sections where electronics are sold and others where books and papers of all kinds can be found.

There is a "Chinatown"; and, yes, that's what they call it. Chinatown is a great place to shop for everything especially during Chinese New Year, February 2nd and 3rd. If you have the great good fortune to be in Singapore during Chinese New Year, Chinatown is a glorious place to be. As one resident put it "She gets all tarted up for the holiday" with banners, joss sticks, fragrant flowers and incense and there are mandarin oranges everywhere, a symbol of good fortune in the new year. You'll find huge malls, all manner of little shops, pushcarts and individuals selling everything for the household, mechanical parts, clothing, jewelry, groceries, rugs, books and much more. Be sure to bargain for the best prices. As with everywhere else in Asia, when you ask "how much" the first price given is merely a starting place. If you don't get a satisfactory offer, turning and walking away - slowly - may get a better one.

Getting Around

Singapore has an impressive ground transportation system. You'll never wait more that 15 minutes for a bus or the underground train, locally referred to as the MRT. The system of payment on the buses is complicated as you are charged by the number of zones, and are required to have exact change. If you overpay there will be no refund. I dealt with this by carrying a lot of change and asking fellow passengers, "dwo shau chen"? The drivers of the buses are not helpful and most either speak no English or pretend not to. There is a helpful source on sale at most bookstands and news kiosks for about fifty cents, entitled "The Bus Guide". There are weekly system-wide passes and other special passes available at very reasonable prices and even the taxis are quite inexpensive.

The taxies here are notorious for not being able to find addresses. They aren't crooked, they just don't know how to find street addresses. Indeed, I once went running in a residential area and became lost in the maze of twisting and turning streets. I was relieved when I came upon a police station after two hours of running in the intense heat. To my chagrin, the police could not direct me back to my starting point even though I had the address. Eventually I found a taxi driver who recognized a water tower I mentioned as visible from the starting point. Once back at that point I had no difficulty directing him to the house where I was staying. You will have no difficulty reaching your destination if you name a hotel, theater or other landmark. Just be sure to determine beforehand whether the taxi driver knows where to go. Finding a taxi in Singapore is no problem, but be prepared to step out into the street and flag one down.

If you wish to fly out of the area, you will save quite a lot by crossing the causeway to Jahore Bahru, Malaysia and flying from there. You can depart Singapore by bus, train or boat. The least expensive way across the causeway to Malaysia is by bus #170, departing Queen Street or Bukit Timah every 15 minutes. The cost is about fifty cents. You may also depart from the Ban Street terminus for the short trip to Johore Bahru on a different bus line for about $1. From the Lavender Street terminus you may depart for Butterworth, the farthest point north in Malaysia, for about $20. If you decide to bus that far, about fourteen hours, be certain your bus has air conditioning or you will have a miserable trip. The Melaka trip by bus takes about five hours and costs less than

$10. Beautiful Penang, on the West Coast, takes fourteen hours on the once daily bus and costs about $20. There are inexpensive tour buses bound for Kuala Lumpur and points north. Morning Star Travel Service, telephone 5342345, 2929009 or 2612688 for the nearest office. Morning Star offers a tour bus to Hat Yai, Thailand for about $25 U.S. Although this service is advertised as "air-conditional (sic) Royal Class V.I.P", I would put it in the same category as a third class bus company in the U.S. It will get you there; just don't expect luxury. You'll hate the toilet facilities in the rest stops!

"Insight Guides - Singapore" published by Prentice Hall in the United States and Canada, is very useful. Be sure to get a copy of The Lonely Planet publication, "Southeast Asia on a Shoestring" or "Malaysia, Singapore & Brunei, a travel survival kit" for more good travel tips on this part of the world. It may be a little out of date, but will still steer you toward some bargains, with weather, money exchange and language tips, as well as interesting things to see.

Malaysia

Eleven of the thirteen states that make up the country known as Malaysia are located on an elongated peninsula stretching from the Thai border to Singapore. Nine of the peninsular states are ruled by sultans. Every five years there are elections to determine which of these sultans will become "Yang di-Pertuan Agong", or King of Malaysia. The parliamentary members are elected, but must be nominated by the King. A prime minister is elected from the parliament. Each of the states also elects a local government, consisting of a chief minister and State Assembly.

Shining beaches, dense jungle, rubber plantations, the oriental splendor of Penang. historical Melaka and bustling Kuala Lumpur all await your discovery. Malaysia offers an extraordinary range of travel experience. Traveling in Malaysia can be a shock to the system after Singapore! Nothing is as clean, efficient or European here. Do not enter this part of the world expecting things to be on schedule, or efficient, or anything like home. Such expectations will ruin an exotic and adventurous experience.

Getting There

Buses and trains are quite inexpensive and fairly easy to arrange. Most of the large Western-style hotels have brochures in the lobby, advertising tour buses and, in any entry port you will find a host of little shops which book cheap train and bus passage.

I was once advised to take a "share taxi" from Jahore Bahru to Kuala Lumpor. I do not recommend this option for any but the bravest among you. To book a share taxi, the traveler pays about $6 U. S., then must wait until four or five most people decide on the same destination. Then, when you are all stuffed into an incredibly elderly Mercedes with broken springs and shocks, the real fun begins. Traffic in Malaysia is the scariest I've experienced. Drivers of buses, taxies, motorcycles and cars play "chicken" and the death toll on their highways reflects the practice. There are posted speed limits, but I do not believe they are observed by anyone. At least when travelling by bus you have more armor to protect you. Fairly often, all traffic into a major city is halted by armed militia, apparently looking for contraband, especially drugs, are dealt with harshly in this part of the world. This should pose no problem for the innocent traveler, except for the interminable delays and discomfort.

Those buses and trains with no air conditioning are miserably hot and humid. Those with air conditioning have one setting - **frigid!** Traveling through Malaysia by train, I found it necessary to put on every item of clothing in my backpack in order to ward off frostbite. I even wound cloth I had purchased around me and put all my socks on my hands and feet, and I was still cold. Don't get me wrong, I love Malaysia for a lot of reasons. I just don't particularly enjoy getting from place to place there.

Housing

There are ample possibilities for low-cost housing, from hostels to Chinese hotels to beach bungalows to camping out. A word of caution: unless you are staying at a place with air-conditioning, be sure to bring bug repellant. If the bugs of the world don't originate here, they must meet here for vacation. One night in Melaka I stayed in a budget hostel without air-conditioning. I went to sleep with the windows open, of course, as it is always hot in Malaysia. I awakened, intensely itchy, turned on the light and found my body literally crawling with an encyclopedic variety of critters. After that, I opted for places with air conditioning so that I could shut the windows.

Unless they belong to Hostelling-International, hostels in Asia are frequently substandard. Wherever you go, people will greet you at the airport, train or bus station, extolling the virtues of their rental housing. Crying "very cheap!" or "best place for you to stay!" they'll actually grab your bags and offer you a free ride. Just don't agree to anything until you've actually inspected the place. If you choose not to stay, expect an argument. Some of these places are terrific and some terrifically awful! Of course you will ask to see the room before you agree to stay. Once again, do not accept the first price offered. When a price is mentioned, offer half, then proceed from there. Sometimes when you ask the price, the concierge counters with "how much can you pay?" In this case, offer a ridiculously low amount and wait for a response.

There are some great places to stay in Malaysia, though, and you can camp out on some of the most beautiful beaches in the world, usually for free if you avoid the tourist traps. Prices are very low for just about everything and if you like the tropics, you'll love Malaysia.

Melaka

Melaka is one of my favorite haunts in Malaysia. It's also spelled "Malacca" and a few other variations, even on official documents. Melaka is certainly the most historically interesting place in Malaysia. To protect this important trade center from perceived enemies, the Siamese and the Moslem religionists, the Malaysians entered into partnership with representatives of the Chinese Ming Dynasty. The Chinese who then migrated to Melaka settled in large numbers and came to be known as "Baba Chinese" or "Straits Chinese". Melaka flourished under Chinese rule, becoming a powerful trading state. The next assault came from the Portuguese, who took over for a time, followed shortly by the Dutch. The Dutch remained in power for 150 years or so until Melaka fell into the hands of the British, where it flourished until occupation by the Japanese during World War II. All of these diverse cultures left interesting relics for you to see in what is now a rather sleepy, laid back town. One way to explore is by trishaw. This cart is pulled by a bicycle, usually pedaled by a Baba Chinese. Agree on a price before you get in. About $5 U.S. should get a daylong tour of all the important landmarks. Be sure to take in Residency Hill to see the ruins of St. Paul's Church and the astonishingly bright pink Christ Church, built by the Dutch and revamped for the British. Although St. Paul's has been in ruins for more than 150 years, the walls and tombstones are still there, marking the reign of the Portuguese and the Dutch. You'll also want to see "Bukit China", which means China Hill. This was once the site of the home of the Sultan of Melaka and his bride, the daughter of the Ming emperor. Nowadays, Bukit China is the largest Chinese burial ground outside of mainland China and it is replete with extraordinary shrines and monuments. Check out the Melaka Museum, too. There is no admission charge and it contains some interesting relics. The Museum is housed in a Dutch dwelling built circa 1660. There is also an extraordinary temple on Jalan Tokong. The oldest in Malaysia, the Cheng Hoon Teng

Chinese temple features the customarily colorful beasts and beings on the roof. Once you enter by way of the massive hardwood doors, you'll find an equally ornate and colorful interior.

Housing in Melaka

There are a number of cheap hostels and reasonably priced Chinese hotels in Melaka. Another traveler had recommended the Malacca Hotel next to the cinema. Finding the entrance to the place was a challenge but once I found it, I looked around and thought it was quite nice. There were good rooms with a fan and attached bathroom for about $6 U.S. Unfortunately there was no room so I moved on to the May Chiang Hotel on Jalan Munshi Abdullah, which was very pleasant and cost about the same. The proprietor is very friendly and helpful. Two thermoses are provided each night, one with hot tea and the other with hot water, which I used for tooth brushing and face washing. I enjoyed the Palace Hotel, also on Munshi Abdullah but farther out of town in the Muar district. It was a little more expensive, about $12 U.S., but the air-conditioning was worth it and the people there were extra nice.

Penang

Penang is the oldest British settlement on the Malay peninsula, actually predating Melaka and Singapore. Although the British found the island virtually uninhabited in 1786, it is unmistakably Chinese.

You'll find remarkable Chinese temples with Hollywood movie-set carvings of dragons, cattle, and warriors depicting an extraordinary history we can only wonder about. There is plenty of inexpensive housing in Georgetown, the largest city on the island. The small Chinese hotels are usually most comfortable and there will quite likely be an English-speaking person available to help you get situated.

The YMCA and the YWCA are safe and cheap, offering single or double accommodations. Both men and women may stay at the YMCA but the YWCA is for women only. I found the YMCA more conveniently located, at 211 Jalan McAlister near the Thai Embassy. Cost is about $10 - slightly more for rooms with air-conditioning. There are also much cheaper dorm beds, but try to get one of the rooms in the back as those in the front are very noisy.

There is a tourist office on Jalan Tun Syed Shah Bearable, where you can purchase "Penang for the Visitor" for about fifty cents. It's well worth it for locating hotels, transportation and local attractions. There are some cheap places to stay at the beach and last I heard, you can still camp out without charge.

Eating in Penang

Eating in Penang, like everywhere in Malaysia, is gastronomic heaven. Fish dishes of all kinds are very popular here, especially Laksa Assam, a fish soup with a tart taste of tamarind (assam) paste. Its usually served with noodles. Laksa Lemak was originally a Thai dish made just like Laksa Assam, except coconut milk is substituted for tamarind. There are many small but artistically appointed Indian restaurants serving spicy curries and the pungent Murtabak, a thin roti chanai pastry stuffed with egg, vegetables and meats. Near the library and cultural center you will find the Seaview Restaurant which features a sumptuous dim sum breakfast and, of course, Chinese restaurants are everywhere.

Kuala Lumpur

When I first traveled to Kuala Lumpur (which is called KL by nearly everyone) I couldn't wait to leave. Arriving by bus into the ugliest part of the city, I found it dirty, smoggy, clogged with motor vehicles of all kinds and positively crawling with humanity. Once explored, however, I found Kuala Lumpur well worth a visit.

The night market in Chinatown provides some excellent bargains and you can find some terrific buys on the back streets throughout the city. Bear in mind that most everything is cheaper here to begin with, and bargaining can be very profitable.

There are many temples and mosques as well as the national museum to visit. The Batu caves are spectacular and certainly worth a special trip, but if you can only see one thing in KL, you absolutely must see the train station. This extraordinary structure, built in 1911, is a strange example of Moorish spires, minarets, cupolas and arches blended with British colonial irony. It appears for all the world like a Hollywood set for a 1940's Arabian Nights movie.

Housing in Kuala Lumpur

I was fortunate to be able to spend the night in the KL Station Hotel, built in the same style as the train station. The price was moderate, about $20 U.S. and my room was enormous. It was sparsely furnished with a bed, cupboard and chair, leaving lots of bare floor space. Hugh double doors opened onto a tiled private balcony from which one could observe the passing scene and listen to the haunting sound of the Moslem call to prayer heard throughout the city. The K.L. Station hotel boasts a lounge, restaurant, pub, hawkers corner, cafeteria and conference room. Sadly, the last I heard, this utterly fascinating hotel may well have been converted to a museum. I hope my information is incorrect, because this place is surely unique in all the world. There are quite a few cheap hostels and Chinese hotels in K.L, but I found the YMCA and YWCA to be the best housing values. Be sure to get a bus pass so that you can see the many interesting sights in K.L. and take advantage of some super shopping.

Genting Highlands

I'm including this popular tourist resort only as a warning. This is a very expensive place. Definitely not a good destination for the budget traveler, Genting Highlands is the home of Malaysia only gambling casino. There are many expensive Western-style hotels, an artificial lake and monstrous golf course. Wealthy folks from all over visit on holiday. My advice is to avoid the place, and if you want to gamble, try Reno, Nevada in the U.S. Another popular tourist spot is **Cameron Highlands,** which is really lovely but regrettably expensive. It is notably cooler and a nice relief from the generally hot and humid climate. Vegetables and flowers are cultivated here for export all over Malaysia due to the Eden-like lush fertility of the area. If you like to explore, you will enjoy the network of jungle tracks, the waterfalls and mountains and the tea plantations welcome visitors.

Shopping in Malaysia

The best bargain I found in Malaysia, was a perfect plum-colored star sapphire. A vendor had set up shop in one of the many dirt alleys in the back streets of Johore Bahru. He had a blanket spread out on the ground upon which were arrayed a number of shallow bowls filled with an assortment of gemstones. It is very difficult, even for an expert, to distinguish between genuine, natural gemstones and man-made imitations. Assuming the sapphire to be synthetic because of the unusual color, I haggled with the man until we agreed upon $10 U.S. My hometown jeweler appraised the value of this genuine stone at $450 U.S. Now, having shared that story with you, I would be remiss if I failed to warn you that there are many fakes being sold in Asia. Indeed, I sought out this same man on another trip and bought some "rubies" from him that proved to be garnets. I took consolation in paying him a price that was quite low for garnets, let alone rubies. If you are interested in buying gems from street vendors, educate yourself first, so that you will recognize quality. Failing that, pay very little so as to lose very little. Consider such purchases a gamble; and like going to Las Vegas, don't spend more than you can afford to lose. One thing that makes gemstone purchase such a bargain in Asia is that you need pay no import duty on unset stones.

Fabrics are a great buy in Malaysia, especially the Malaysian Batik, which is quite different from the more familiar Indonesian variety. Another unusual fabric available here is Kain Songket cloth. You'll also find unusual wooden craft items, wickerwork silver and brasswork. Tops, the kind one spins, are serious adult business in this country. They can weigh up to seven kilograms, requiring adult strength to spin. Top spinning is a very popular sport and contests are held regularly. The Malaysians are also famous for their fantastic kites, which have to be seen to be appreciated. Unfortunately, they are difficult to pack and carry away with you.

Eating in Malaysia

Ahhhhh, eating in Malaysia! The most delectable fruits in the world come from this wonderful place, and, for the most part, they are in season all year long. The Malaysians have a way with cooking that will please the most jaded palate. Of course, you will also find spicy Thai and all the varieties of Chinese cuisine as well as Middle Eastern, Indonesian and Indian fare. The water is not drinkable, though, so you must rely on bottled water, juices and other beverages. I was warned not even to brush my teeth with tap water. I forgot, of course, but suffered no ill effects from that slight exposure.

Remember when you visit Malaysia that this is a Moslem country. Women are expected to be decorous and modest in their clothing and behavior. Once past my feminist outrage at such a policy, I did not find it a hardship to conform and I believe I was more comfortable in the long run.

Running In Malaysia

Speaking of running, I discovered while running a hot, humid, hilly 10 kilometer race that water is not provided in any foot race of less distance than a half marathon. So runners beware, and carry water with you! You will not find women runners wearing shorts outside of big cities. I adapted with some difficulty to running in sweat pants, despite the heat and humidity. Competing in Kuala Lumpur's traditional Pesta Larian New Year's Day race, I was amused by the variety of attired favored by the participants. Some wore saris and sandals, others were clad in the latest singlets and shorts. There were young women in frilly dresses and men wearing traditional middle eastern garb. There were bare feet and Nikes, dress shoes and hiking boots. Even if running is not your cup of tea, watching such events provides fascinating insight into a culture.

Thailand

If you are planning a trip to Thailand, I recommend that you first purchase a book entitled "Thailand - a travel survivor kit". You will find it at your local bookstore or you can have them order it for you. This book provides very useful information on transportation, housing, language, culture, and much more; and will serve you very well in planning your trip. Stay loose, though. Remember when you travel in Asia, you should have plan A, plan B for when A doesn't pan out, and plan C when all else fails, wing it!

As a practical matter, you may reach Thailand via courier flights directly into Bangkok, or you may travel overland through

Malaysia. Any other route will either consume a lot of time or money, and may not be safe. Thailand is user-friendly for the economically disadvantaged. The American dollar has been stable there for some time at about 25.50 bahts, and housing and food are plentiful and cheap, especially if you stay away from the main tourist areas. The people are quite friendly and hospitable and the food is legendary - like Chinese with a fiery accent.

Phuket on the East coast, is a good example of the kind of place to avoid. Once a serenely lovely island, unspoiled and inexpensive, Phuket is now mostly overrun with tourists and those who make their livelihood from tourists. It still has many charms, but in my opinion, pales in comparison with Koh Samui on the West coast.

Koh Samui

Koh Samui in Southwestern Thailand is relatively quiet and off the beaten path. "Koh" in the Thai language means island. The best approach here is to enter Thailand from Malaysia by bus, train or taxi from Butterworth in Malaysia to Ban Don, Thailand. As of this writing, the only access to the island is by water, and that apparently discourages many tourists. To get there, take one of two daily boats from Ban Don. The journey takes from two and one half to three hours. Try to get on the upper deck for the view. Even though there are no seats or benches, you can stretch out and lie on the deck if you like. Be sure to remove your shoes. This is the custom and it is a practical measure to prevent scarring the highly polished deck. Once on the island, the mode of transport is the "song taos", small pickup trucks which will taxi you around for a laughably small amount of money. Most of the bungalows and shops also have light motorbikes you can rent for a pittance.

Koh Samui is separate from mainland Thailand in more than just geography. The people there call themselves "chao samui", which means Samui folk, rather than Thais. Chao samui are renowned for their friendliness and sense of humor.

Koh Samui Housing and Food

Housing is especially attractive to the budget-minded traveler, as there are a large number of beach bungalows available at astonishingly low prices. If you must stay in the largest town on the island, Na Thawn (alternatively spelled Na Thon) has a number of hotels priced from cheap to moderate. Personally, I prefer the ambience of the family-owned beach bungalows. There are nearly a dozen of these to choose from, ranging in price from $3 up. Sak's Bungalows is a favorite with the budget traveler. Clean, cheap an fairly quiet, the proprietor loans books and snorkeling equipment for the asking. Moon Bungalows is newer, and a little more upscale, going for about $7. There are several other wonderful, thatched roof bungalows I can heartily recommend. The Big Buddha and the Family Village both have decks overlooking the ocean and the cost is less than $6.

Food is distinctive on the island, reflecting the economic realities. Coconut export is the main source of income of the inhabitants, around two million tons are shipped to Bangkok monthly. Because of the ubiquitous coconut palm, much of the cuisine is flavored with the tasty fruit. Langat, durian and rambutan are also cultivated, and I would recommend that you sample these. Fish dishes are prevalent, as you would expect in a tropical island setting.

There is a great French restaurant called L'Auberge just past Lamai on the road to Chawing. The food is a perfect marriage of French and Thai, the service is remarkable, the hosts are charming and your meal is relatively inexpensive. You'll find great food all over the place, especially at the View Star and the Best Beach Cafe.

The beauty and charm of the place, the warmth of the people, the simplicity of the life is such that Koh Samui has become my favorite destination in Thailand.

Eating in Thailand

Eating in Thailand is one of life's most joyous experiences. My attempts to master any useful bits of the language were unfruitful and few restaurants outside of the main tourist areas offer English menus. "Thailand - a travel survival kit" offers a list of Thai dishes described in English with Thai language to show your server. If you are wise you will also arm yourself with the leaflet "Eating in Thailand" available at most government tourist offices. This useful paper lists many common foods with English descriptions and Thai script; so all you need do is find something that sounds appealing and point to the written Thai. This doesn't always work, as I have discovered many food servers who can't (or won't) read it. I found it best to point at this dish or that, indicating with sign language (dramatically fanning my tongue) that I preferred mild seasoning. I found to my chagrin that the Thai conception of mild was spicy enough to cause my eyes and nose to run profusely. Either that or I underestimated the Thai sense of humor. Watch out for "phrik kii noo" literally translated as "mouse shit peppers". These tiny dark brown peppers are named for their appearance and their heat would melt an igloo! Be prepared to improvise. You can't go wrong with fruit, and Thailand is blessed with the most remarkably varied and delicious fruit in the world.

Shopping in Thailand

Night markets in Thailand, indeed throughout Asia, offer all manner of bargains. I believe you could buy almost anything at these street fairs including sex and other sinful activities, which, of course, I cannot recommend from personal experience. Sellers will approach you in every public place offering "copy watches" and other goods; and you will find carts, flimsy tables and tarpaulins covered with every imaginable (and occasionally unimaginable) item for purchase.

You can find wonderful fabrics at great prices on cotton, batik and gorgeous Thai silk. You'll also find silks from China and India at good prices, but watch out for synthetics! There are interesting crafts, jewelry, handbags and ornaments and you can buy amulets to protect you from every conceivable misfortune. Thailand is an antique collectors dream come true. There are extraordinarily beautiful, curious, exotic and absolutely unique relics available for purchase everywhere in Thailand. Let the buyer beware, though, as there are a lot of fakes, too. To be absolutely certain it's the real thing, buy only at shops that honor your Visa, American Express or Mastercard. That way your purchase is insured against fraud. Designer-label rip-offs are everywhere and some are, at first glance, indistinguishable from the real thing. These are very cheap and they should be because most won't hold up for long. Colors run and fade. Seams unravel and clothing shrinks into the most peculiar shapes. I bought a cotton "Nike" singlet complete with a tag claiming Beaverton, Oregon, U.S.A. manufacture. I knew better because of the quality, but needed something cool to wear so I "blew" about 10 cents on the purchase.

If you are in an area that attracts tourists, you'll have to bargain extra hard. Wealthy or careless tourists don't bargain, thus driving up the asking prices. If you have qualms about bargaining, just remember this is a local custom and is expected. Asking prices are usually inflated to allow for a spirited debate in which you offer a ridiculously low amount and then buyer and seller meet in the middle. In this system, both parties can feel a sense of accomplishment; the buyer for getting a terrific bargain and the seller for having made a reasonable profit. Each comes away from the transaction gleefully believing he has gotten the better of the other fellow. Don't worry, the seller won't get less than a reasonable profit!

Bangkok

There is, of course much more to Thailand. I have omitted most detail on Bangkok because I am not comfortable in that city. The extraordinary poverty of many of the inhabitants makes me feel that I am exploiting them and the crash and grind of the city with its teeming millions exhausts me. "Thailand - a travel survival kit" gives lots of current information on Bangkok and there are many other guidebooks on the market that will tell you all you will need to know about that city. If you arrive in Bangkok by air, you can go into the city via Thai Airways bus to downtown. You purchase the bus ticket for about $4.00 at Thai Limousine Service desk outside the customs hall. Alternatively, you can take a cab operated by Thai International Airways, purchasing a ticket at their desk outside customs. It will take about 20 minutes to get to town.

There is ample cheap, relatively comfortable housing available. I would particularly recommend the four Bangkok youth hostels that belong to the International Youth Hostel Association. They are safe, clean and meet the standards required to belong to the association. You will find specifics in the publication "Budget Accommodations - Africa, America, Asia, Australasia" published by the International Youth Hostel Federation.

Chiang Mai

In the far north of Thailand the temperature reflects changing seasons. The "coldest" month is January, The term "cold" is relative, as the coldest temperature ever recorded in Northern Thailand was 42.8 Fahrenheit, which was recorded in the north. The hottest temperature on record was 106.7 F. By March the weather is warm with low humidity and is very pleasant. April is the hottest month, and the rains come in torrents from June to the end of September. The best time to visit is November through February when nights are cool and days bright, sunny and dry.

Chiang Mai, over 700 kilometers northwest of Bangkok, is 19 degrees north of the equator and is an important major province, containing the capitol city of the same name. The city is on a flat, rice plain about 1000 feet above sea level and is roughly two-thirds surrounded by mountains, called "Doi" in the Thai language.

Getting To and Around Chiang Mai

You can easily reach Chiang Mai from Bangkok by bus, train or air. If you elect the train, I suggest a sleeper. It's a long trip, taking up to 16 hours. And that's the express train! If you are travelling in the hot season, be certain that bus or train is air-conditioned. Failing that, make sure your berth is on the east side as this is the coolest in both directions. Train fare will be from 200 bahts up. The bus is definitely faster (about nine hours) and cheaper (starting at 150 bahts and up). You can get the bus at Mor Chit Market on Phahonyothin Road.

Getting around in Chiang Mai is easy and cheap. Local buses cost less than 5 baht per 10 kilometers. Keep in mind that the exchange rate has remained stable for a very long time at 25.5 bahts to the dollar. Nearly as cheap and much more enjoyable is the pedal samlor, rather like the trishaw of Malaysia. The quickest way around is the motor samlor, which was called a tuk tuk because of the sound it made. These are three or four wheeled minicabs cost about the same as the bus or the pedal samlor. Now, I've heard tuk tuks are being replaced by an electric vehicle, so the sound will, alas, be no more. I don't know if they'll change the name. Of the three, the pedal samlor is best for sightseeing, as the driver is likely to be an interesting character who will act as guide. Many speak English and are knowledgeable and helpful. When you stop to eat, invite the driver to have a meal with you; your treat, of course. Ask the driver to suggest good places to shop that are not expensive. I have found them to be extremely valuable allies in the pursuit of a bargain. One warning about samlor drivers in Chiang Mai - They have a reputation for selling drugs to tourists and then turning them in to the police. The police then levy stiff fines or, if the tourist can't pay what amounts to a bribe, jail time. I never had this or any other problem with drivers, but felt I had to pass on the warning.

Strolling around the old city, you will find many ornate temples, called Wats, fascinating shops and other wonders, including a museum full of interesting antiquities, arts and crafts. The city itself is neatly contained in a square surrounded by moats.

Shopping in Chiang Mai

The night market, or night bazaar, is an experience not to be missed. Always exciting and energetic, during special festivals it is the center of activity, not to mention a great place for shopping. In fact, many importers come to the Chiang Mai night bazaar to buy the goods they will sell in large cities around the world. Clothing of all kinds can be found at incredibly low prices if you are willing to bargain. Hand-woven fabrics can be purchased as yard goods or made up with skill into clothing for men, women and children. There is a special shoulder bag, called a "yaam". Ceramic production is a tradition here, and if you are so inclined you can visit the most famous producer, Thai Celadon Kilns, 8 kilometers out of town. Silver, brass and carved wooden ware are beautiful and cheap. Chiang Mai is noted for lacquer ware. You will also find Burmese lacquer ware in the market. My favorite purchase in Thailand was a "phaasin", an all-purpose length of cloth used like a sarong, wrapped around the head as a turban, used as a sheet or tablecloth, used to wrap things in and hundreds of other uses. The male version of this handy stuff is called phaakma. Oddly enough, the female version is the larger of the two. When purchasing wearing apparel, always fit for size. Asian people are very small. Although I generally wear things marked "extra small" at home, in Asia I am usually a medium and occasionally large. If you are interested in seeing or buying tribal hill crafts, go to Thai Tribal Crafts, 208 Bamrung Road. It is a non-profit facility run by two churches and you will get the best possible buy there as well as excellent selection and quality. You will want to go out to Baw Sang village, nine kilometers east of Chiang Mai, to see all the crafts - especially the umbrellas. The whole village consists of craft shops and the umbrellas manufactured here are legendary.

Housing in Chiang Mai

There are two approved youth hostels in Chiang Mai. The city hostel is at 21/8 Chang Clan Road, Mooban OON-RUEN, Chiang Mai 5000, telephone 053/276-737. The cost is from 50-300 baht depending upon the type of accommodation you require. The other hostel is in Chang Pauk at 4 Ratchapaknai Road, Prs Sing Sub-district, telephone 053/272-169. There are quite a few inexpensive guesthouses and hotels in the area. I especially liked the Je T'aime Guest House at 247-9 Charoen Rat Road. It is a little removed from town, but they will arrange to pick you up if you telephone 234-912. Every room has a fan and a private shower and I found it to be clean and quiet. For more housing recommendations, check "Thailand - a travel survival kit".

Eating in Chiang Mai

There is no shortage of good food, here. I've heard and I believe that excluding Bangkok, the best restaurants in Thailand are in Chiang Mai. If you are craving Western food, you'll find it at Daret Restaurant on Moon Mooang Road. They also whip up a mean fruit smoothie. There's a place called Serimit on the road to San Kamphaeng just across from Poy Luang Hotel that serves great Thai food - personal favorite phak je maw din, fresh veggies steamed in a clay pot. I found this place through "Thailand - a travel survival kit". Usually you will do well following their suggestions. The same publication recommends three vegetarian restaurants that I found to be excellent, the aptly named Vegetarian Restaurant served tasty Thai dishes and was very cheap. The

Whole Earth Restaurant was a little more expensive but offered excellent Indian Vegetarian Foods. You will find a lot of good Chinese food here, and there are some excellent noodle shops where you can always find a quick, delicious meal at a very reasonable price. There are many seafood and chicken specialties here and you might want to sample Burmese cuisine, available in a number of places.

Hong Kong

Hong Kong cannot easily be described. This is primarily because you can literally find whatever you're looking for here. Most of Hong Kong is a seething cauldron of humanity; of every race, color and religion. Incredibly rich and heartbreakingly poor inhabitants squeeze through the crowds, shoulder to shoulder. Driven financial yuppies, vile sex peddlers, devout clergy and desperate drug addicts share the teeming streets, sidewalks and alleys with wealthy tourists and scruffy backpackers of the world. Most of these more than five million souls are crowded into Hong Kong Island, Kowloon and New Kowloon. The entire colony covers only 1034 square kilometers and much of the land is sparsely inhabited. The Chinese government resumed control of Hong Kong in 1997, and it is certain there will be some kind of upheaval. They have assured the world that it will not change, but change it must, politically, economically and socially. Either the Chinese will change Hong Kong or Hong Kong will change the Chinese. At any rate, if you have the opportunity to go there, don't miss it, and who knows, perhaps Hong Kong will triumph.

The average tourist sees very little of the real Hong Kong. Tour operators book travelers into the many opulent and expensive western-style hotels; then escort their charges through the most sanitized parts of Hong Kong. Victoria Peak, where most of the wealthiest families in Hong Kong live, the Tiger Balm Gardens, the Jade Market, the night clubs and the cruises around the colonies are all interesting and worth seeing, but there is much more to Hong Kong than these glitzy tourist haunts. One can shop the fine stores on Nathan Road, which rival those of Rodeo Drive in Beverly Hills for glamour and expense; or go three or four blocks away and buy the designer labels directly from the manufacturer or from a push cart in the street for a pittance. I once purchased three cashmere sweaters for $10. These garments were identical in every respect to those selling for $150 on Nathan Road - well made name brands all. Housing can cost $200 and up per night in decadent splendor or $8 in a crowded backpackers dormitory (or absolutely nothing if you are prepared to camp out in a more remote location). This housing is likely to be next door or right across the street. Unlike other ventures in other places, location means very little in Hong Kong.

When you first arrive at Hong Kong's Kai Tak airport, you will find a wealth of information at hand in the airport. Leaflets and booklets with every imaginable bit of information you will need are free for the taking. Among these you will find lists of youth hostels as well as more upscale housing. The usual tourist attractions are described in loving detail, as well as the more obscure and exotic, lesser known landmarks and places of interest. If you don't get every bit of information you need here, don't despair. You can go to the Hong Kong Tourist Association for anything else you might need. They have offices all over the territory.

If you haven't any Hong Kong currency with you, you will need to change some in the airport. $200 Hong Kong dollars (about $25 U.S.) will be enough to cover ground transportation, a meal and a bed for the night, leaving something for the morning. You can get a taxi or take a bus right outside the airport. A taxi would cost about $10 or $12 U.S. Take bus A1 to the Holiday Inn Golden Mile and you will be in the heart of the cheapest and most expensive hotels. You need exact change; as of this writing $8 HK, about $1 U.S. There's a place for your luggage as you enter the bus. I've never had a problem with theft in this situation, but then I sit where I can see it just to be sure.

Housing

As you wait for transport, you will probably be approached by an assortment of people offering cheap accommodations. Some will even offer a ride. It probably is a better idea to determine where you need to go while you are still in the airport and telephone to make arrangements. Local calls are about five cents, U.S., and you can call from the list you have obtained from the Hong Kong Tourist Association kiosk in the airport. After the long, arduous flight to Hong Kong, it's likely going to be a good idea to splurge a bit on your first night. Also, unless you arrive early in the day, it will be impossible to reach the better hostel accommodations, as most are far from the airport.

When you leave the bus, directly in front of the Holiday Inn, you will be virtually next door to Chungking Mansions. That sounds really grand, I know, but do not be deceived. "Mansion" in this part of the world just means living space; and the spaces here range from rather nice to rat warren. Chungking Mansions occupies a huge city block. The lower floors offer a zillion shops and small restaurants selling just about everything. Within, there are four "blocks" which are identified by the alphabet, and you must find the correct elevator (called a "lift" hereabouts) in order to access the block you are seeking. You cannot traverse from one block to another. Ask for directions. Most people here speak some English, or will point you to someone who can. Don't be too put off by the lifts. They are awfully small, nearly always crammed and you nearly always have to wait for them. Usually, more people try to squeeze in than allowable, but a buzzer sounds and the lift will not proceed until the load is shifted or someone gets off. Once, when I was staying on the 17th floor (called a "storey") the lift was full of non-English speaking people from the top down. Because this was a busy time of day, it stopped at each storey down and people tried to get in. On impulse, I muttered "no way, Jose" on the 13th storey, and from there down, everyone in the lift chanted the same at each stop, laughing all the way. I doubt they knew specifically what the words meant, but all got the idea, and perceived it as hilarious.

As crowded as the lifts are, the stairways are some of the worst in the world. In spite of the fact that they are diligently scrubbed every morning, they become unimaginably filthy and smelly as the day progresses. Fortunately (or perhaps not?) they are also dimly lit, so you cannot see the cockroaches and other critters!

Having said all that, many of the guesthouses occupying Chungking Mansions are extremely clean and well kept. Some have air-conditioning, telephone, private toilet and shower. Some are pretty awful, so you will want to inspect your room before you agree to stay, regardless of the appearance of the reception area. I can recommend the Welcome Guesthouse on the 7th storey of C Block, The cost for a private room will be about $15 to $20 U.S. In A Block, the New Mandarin on the 8th storey costs about $20 for the same type of accommodation. If you want the cheapest available night's sleep, you can get a dorm bed at the Traveler's Hostel on the 17th storey of A Block for $40 HK. That's a little less than $5 U.S. There are cooking facilities, clean toilets and individual showers. There's a television in the common room where you can catch the local or BBC world news or an old American TV series re-run or movie. The local stations are mostly broadcast in Cantonese, but there is at least one English-language station. Traveler's management is friendly and helpful. They will exchange a small amount of money at a fair rate for you if you need it. You will find a residents offering used guidebooks and novels for sale cheap. There is a bulletin board in the reception area on which you will find notices selling all kinds of useful stuff, including Chinese currency, which you will need if you plan to go there. For a small fee, Traveler's will also store baggage for you when you want to travel on lightly. Usually, though, I find someone in my dorm, willing to keep an eye on my things while I'm away. It's best to use one of the small lockers for anything of value. I carry a padlock with me for this purpose. There is no charge for the locker while you are staying there.

Traveler's Hostel is often my headquarters when in Hong Kong, except when it is very crowded or during the hottest, most humid time of year. Then it is really miserable! Everyone smokes in the common rooms and it is difficult get into the kitchen to cook at any normal mealtime. Even that time of year, I have found it a useful place to find another single traveler with whom I can share expense in a nicer, cooler environment. Elsewhere in Chungking Mansions, there are double rooms with air-conditioning costing $80 HK and up, and there is no difference in the price for two people. You can use the telephone at Traveler's to call around to other guesthouses; but be sure to inspect the premises before you decide where to move.

If you want to get out of Chungking Mansions, and you want rock-bottom prices and less crowded circumstances, try Victoria Hostel where a bed in a four person dormitory goes for less than $10 U.S. Hong Kong is full of relatively cheap guesthouses and I refer you to the Lonely Planet publication, "Hong Kong, Macau & Canton" for a comprehensive listing. Most likely the prices quoted will be a little out of date but it will serve as a guide. Rule of thumb, add about half to the price listed. There are a few youth hostels that belong to the international association and thus meet the standards. These are listed in the HKTA pamphlet you get in the airport and in the publications of the International Youth Hostel Association. It's a good idea to call ahead to reserve a bed and get directions as some are in remote locations.

Lantau Island

My favorite place to stay when visiting Hong Kong is on Lantau Island. Sadly, I understand that a new airport will be constructed there soon. I do not know at this writing what that will mean for the environment and housing; only time will tell.

Be mindful of the fact that the ferries run from 6:15 a.m. until 10 p.m. There are 18 to 20 ferries from Hong Kong to Silvermine Bay (Mui Wo) daily. Once there, you take bus #2 all the way up to Po Lin Monastery, continue walking up the mountain past the Lantau Tea Gardens and follow the signs to the S.G. Davis Youth Hostel. You can stay at Po Lin Monastery for $100 HK, or with three simple but excellent vegetarian meals for $130 HK. The Tea Garden has simple accommodations for $120 HK, but really isn't anything special. The hostel will cost about $35 HK (less than $5 U.S.). You can also camp out for free with permission. If you camp, you will be allowed to use the showers, toilets and cooking facilities in the hostel; making this the most cost-effective stay in the region. It's absolutely beautiful with a breathtaking view, located at the highest point on the island. There is a well-established footpath going all the way down to the bottom, but don't try it unless the weather is cool and you are very fit. As one who has completed an 88-mile run in a 24-hour period, I was able to finish this walk without any great difficulty; but I wouldn't recommend it to a tenderfoot. There is much to see along the way and I do recommend that you walk along the path until you are a little tired, stop and rest a while, then return to your starting point. At various points on the way down the mountain, you will find old stone dwellings within little villages and remote shrines and people living in ways relatively untouched by modern life, unchanged for centuries. Sadly, the beach at Silvermine bay is usually littered and crowded with day trippers from Hong Kong, but you can go for a swim if you like. Another interesting and unusual place to stay on Lantau is on the other side of the island. I have hiked the approximately 20 kilometers over the top, following a sketchy footpath known as the Lantau Trail, but it takes a long time and would be very difficult with luggage. (Oddly, I came across a 1955 to 1960 Chevrolet convertible up there, miles from any real road. I never found out what it was doing there, but guess it might have been a movie prop.) You can get a map of the trail and other walks in the vicinity of Hong Kong from the HKTA offices. There is no other land route. You can most easily get there by taking the ferry to Peng Chau. The monastery's boat meets every ferry and takes passengers on to their dock. There is a very modern appearing road from the dock to the monastery, about two miles uphill. I saw no motor vehicles, so the road is another puzzle. The monastery charges $80 Hong Kong for a bed and three simple meals, generally whatever the monks eat. Most of the monks take a vow of silence and all observe silence after 10 p.m., so it's a very restful place to stay especially after the noise and hustle of Hong Kong.

Shopping in Hong Kong

The night markets in Hong Kong, as everywhere in Asia, offer a veritable feast of bargains in everything from food to cellular phones. As an aside, you will notice an extraordinary number of ordinary looking individuals speaking into their cell phones as they scurry through Hong Kong's maze of streets. Some of the best bargains are found in the pushcarts, which are illegal in Hong Kong. This illegality doesn't seem to trouble anyone very much. Periodically the vendors, at some imperceptible cue, cover their wares and scuttle off to another street. When this happens, the police invariably turn up, just missing the carts. The vendors then set up shop and conduct business as usual from another spot nearby. When I've questioned these entrepreneurs about the practice, they shrug and say something like "Mai wun chee", no problem! I've never observed the police catching anyone, but I suppose they sometimes do, and fines are probably levied.

Bargaining is the byword throughout Asia and Hong Kong is no exception. Even if you don't speak the language, just follow the procedure outlined in the section on Singapore, and you'll do fine. The language usually spoken here is Cantonese, but they seem to understand bargaining words in Mandarin.

For great daytime shopping, take the MRT (Underground train) from Chungking Mansions to the Mong Kok station. This is probably where most of the residents of Hong Kong buy their everyday goods. Some blocks sell nothing but engine parts, others building supplies, but you will find just about anything you could possible want here - clothes, books, food, electronics, dishes, etc. You will also find some great little food stands rather like hawker stands in Singapore. In Hong Kong and China they are called "dai pai dongs".

Another great place to shop is Central district on Hong Kong Island which you can reach via the MRT, by bus, or you can take a ferry. All modes of ground transportation are very cheap and there are special tickets for weekly or excursion use. These are on sale in all the MRT Stations. The street markets in Central are the best bet, rather than the shops, which tend to be rather expensive. You'll find inexpensive yardgoods on Wing On Street, known locally as Cloth Alley. Another alley offers only leather goods, another will have dresses and so on. Specializing is an art form here.

You'll find ivory on sale all over Hong Kong, but don't buy it. It is illegal to bring ivory into the U.S. and many other countries. Jade is also everywhere and can be had for excellent prices if you know how to determine quality. There is a huge "tent city" that the locals call "the Jade Market" where you will find an astonishing variety of jade in all prices, qualities and colors. I have purchased Nike running shoes for about half the U.S. price, but I had to bargain strenuously. Since most athletic shoes are assembled in Asia, the prices are rather low compared to North America. I've found good buys in camera equipment, film and various electronics, especially watches and radios. I never buy more than I can reasonably take back home in my carry-on luggage, as it is extremely expensive to ship anything. I found a real bonanza in some pseudo-antique silver dollars in Hong Kong. They were not real antiques, but they were really silver, and I purchased them for much less than the value of the silver content.

Recreation and Entertainment in Hong Kong

Until you've been to Victoria Peak, you have not seen Hong Kong. At least that's what every guidebook says, so this will not be the exception. The view on a clear day really is magnificent and the finest homes in the colony are located here. It's also a great place for a run, with trails that average two and a half miles per circuit and feature a marvelous view, especially at sunrise and sunset. There is a running track in Victoria Park. The best place to run in all of Hong Kong is on the peak at Harlech Lugard Roads. The peak has been the best address in Hong Kong since the Taipans claimed it and is still considered a refuge for the privileged.

If you are a night person, there is a lot to love in Hong Kong. There are lots of bars, nightclubs, pubs and theaters. Karaoke is very popular at the moment, so if you sing well or like to watch other amateurs, this is for you. There are some truly amazing female impersonators here. As a woman, I was intimidated! These are some of the loveliest creatures I've ever seen, regardless of their chromosome configurations!

Each morning at dawn you will find practitioners of Tai Chi Chuan in every park in Asia. This graceful art form has been practiced by the Chinese for centuries and remains extremely popular today. I learned the basics by simply joining in as many of these sessions as possible. As far as I could determine, there is no charge for participation except in the very few cases where a fee is prominently posted.

If you like to swim, there is a large, free municipal pool in Kowloon Park. This appears to be a carefully guarded secret I happened to stumble upon on my fifth trip to Hong Kong. It's a real Godsend on a hot, humid summer day. At first I thought there was a charge for admission, as the attendant asked me for a small sum, but this is just a returnable key deposit for your locker. Kowloon Park is nice, but I understand only a shadow of its former self. It remains a shady, peaceful spot in the midst of a bustling city. The Kowloon Museum of History is located in the park and is also free. Enter the park from the Haiphong Road entrance for the Museum.

You will find the impressive Kowloon Mosque nearby. You are free to admire it from the outside, but cannot enter without permission, which I understand is not freely given. Gambling seems to be a Chinese passion. Betting on Mahjong is especially popular and wherever you go in Asia, you can hear the clacking of Mahjong tiles accompanied by laughter and shouts. Although horseracing was introduced to Hong Kong by the British, the Chinese adopted it with great enthusiasm, and the track at Happy Valley is always crowded to the rafters. I understand there is a newer and nicer track in Shatin in the New Territories. It is also my understanding that this is an extremely expensive bit of entertainment; although I have no personal experience by which to judge.

There are many day tours available. Among these are harbor cruises of varying length and expense. The Hong Kong harbor is surely one of the most magnificent sights in the world. The sheer size of it is awesome. Docked in the harbor in stupefying numbers is every imaginable kind of water craft from nearly every nation in the world. Tiny little bumboats, serving as home and workplace for large families share the murky waters with jet-set yachts, fast moving hovercraft, huge tankers and passenger ferries. If you so desire, you can find a very reasonably priced lunch or dinner cruise; but you will have to do some comparison shopping around.

Another worthwhile free attraction in Hong Kong is the Zoological and Botanical Garden in which you will find hundreds of exotic species of birds and plants. There's also a very nice running trail there. My personal favorite entertainment in Hong Kong involves sampling the extraordinary cuisine from all over the world.

Eating in Hong Kong

In the English language one is frequently greeted politely with the words "how are you?" This does not necessarily reflect genuine interest in one's health. Just so, in the Chinese language, you can greet someone with the rhetorical question, "nee hau ma?" which means "how are you?" or you might inquire, equally rhetorically, "Nee chir la ma?" meaning "have you eaten yet?" The greeting is a good indicator of the degree to which food is appreciated in Asia.

From the dai pai dong, where a hearty meal of rice, vegetables, meat and tea will cost less than $2 US, to a sumptuous ten-course banquet in an elegant setting with impeccable white gloved service for $150 - you can find everything at every price in Hong Kong, and that includes the food. For the traveler on a budget, you can't beat the dai pai dong. Just a small warning; sanitary conditions do not measure up the U.S. standards. I was stricken with food-borne illness only once in all of my travels. As near as I can tell, the vegetables I consumed in a dai pai dong were brought in from Southwestern China where they were contaminated with pesticides. This provided my introduction to the Hong Kong Medical Community. I will elaborate on this in the section "General Tips for the Traveler". It is my understanding that people all over Hong Kong became ill from these vegetables, including those who dined at fine restaurants. Generally, the food is so good that it's worth whatever small risk one might incur. For the best value meals in Hong Kong, the many dai pai dongs just can't be beat. Just follow the locals at mealtime, go in and just point at whatever looks good to you then sit down and wait. Usually a meal will cost $2 or $3 U.S.

You will find some wonderful and inexpensive Indian food on the third storey of C Block in Chungking Mansions. The Delhi Club serves a superb complete meal for about $3 US. They will deliver to your room free of charge if you telephone 3681682.

There's also good Italian food available at the Spaghetti house on Cameron Road at comparable prices. You can get a cheap American-style breakfast at Cherikoff's at 184 Nathan Road, but my favorite breakfast when really hungry is at the YMCA at Waterloo Road. As a vegetarian, I adore buffet meals where I can really pig out on the fresh fruit, potatoes, porridge, rice and toast. For meat eaters, they also serve eggs, fish, bacon and sausage. The YMCA at Waterloo charges about $5 U.S. for this "all-you-can-eat" repast, which includes fresh juice and wonderful coffee. Although this is more than I usually budget for a meal, I generally indulge at least once on every trip. The Salisbury YMCA does not serve a comparable meal and is much more expensive. When staying at a hostel, you can bring food in and prepare it yourself for real economy, splurging on cooked food whenever the budget allows. Hong King is full of supermarkets and street markets where you can purchase foods at a reasonable price.

For a really special dining experience, be sure to try the vegetarian meals served at the Po Lin Monastery. If you do not stay there, you can purchase a three- meal ticket for about $10 U.S. Your ticket will specify a table number. At mealtimes you enter the meal hall and find your table. About eight people are seated at each table and all meals are served family style, sharing whatever is served. First you take your bowl to an enormous community rice steamer and help yourself to as much as you like, refilling whenever you wish. Remember, though, it is considered very bad form to leave any rice uneaten, so don't take more than you can eat. The food is basic, simple and delicious. Food servers bring out many different bowls of prepared vegetables and some of tofu. The tofu is marvelously prepared to look and taste like chicken and/or pork, fish or beef and is quite good. The only meal I did not enjoy was breakfast, as Chinese breakfast is an acquired taste that I've not acquired. Chinese breakfast is a soupy rice - imagine cooking rice with too much water and you have the picture. Non-vegetarians supplement this with tiny pieces of pork, chicken or fish.

Macau

Before going there, my total awareness of Macau was limited to a few black and white "B" movies from the 40's. I particularly remember one darkly glamorous film, starring Jane Russell and Robert Mitchum. It had a forgettable plot set against a background of piracy, gambling, drugs and assorted illicit activities. The truth is actually more interesting than any fictionalized account. Macau has always been a Chinese territory. It was leased to the adventurous Portuguese by the Ming Emperor Yong Le, circa 1556, supposedly in exchange for ridding the area of marauding pirates who had plagued the area for centuries. Because Chinese traders were forbidden from going abroad under penalty of death, they needed the services of the Portuguese, The Portuguese were only too happy to oblige, enriching themselves in the process. From that time Macau thrived as a major world trade center. Macau also became a center of Christianity in the Far East. Priests and missionaries mixed with the traders on Portuguese ships bound for Macau, creating a strange mix of the devout and the profane. These groups were often at crossed purposes but managed to settle into a long term marriage of convenience.

Some splendid baroque churches were built, most notably the awe-inspiring Basilica of Sao Paulo, which was rightly called the greatest monument of Christianity in the East. The facade of this structure is all that remains today. High on a hill overlooking Macau, this peculiar relic gives only a hint of Macau's colorful history. Just a little higher on the same hill is a fortress, ancient cannon still guarding the harbor against ghostly pirates. As the Dutch and the Japanese rose in the world trading arena, Portugal began its decline and by 1841, when the British took control of Hong Kong, the party was over. Until the mid-19th century,

Portugal, China and the British squabbled over dominion of Macao. In 1887, China granted recognition of Portuguese sovereignty. Japan recognized Portuguese neutrality in World War I so Macau was not invaded. With China and Hong Kong under attack by the Japanese, Macau became a haven for threatened refuges throughout Asia and the population burgeoned to 500,000.

After suffering various difficulties with the Communist Chinese, a military coup put an effective end to Portuguese dominion in Macau. Finally, in March of 1987, Portugal and China signed an agreement to the effect that Macau will be a Special Administrative Region of China for 50 years after 20 December 1999. This agreement is similar to the pact between Britain the China as regards Hong Kong, which will revert to the Chinese in 1997. Unlike the people of Hong Kong, who will not automatically become British citizens, residents of Macau may continue to hold Portuguese passports if they wish.

Macau is a small island, with a landmass of only 16 square kilometers. Having been there, I am certain that 95% of the land not covered by a building of some kind is covered with automobiles. Said automobiles park with impunity wherever the driver pleases regardless of posted regulations, even on the sidewalks. This makes Macau quite inhospitable to the hapless pedestrian. Gambling is the most visible source of income on the island, although I'm told there are a variety of light industries that thrive because of very low wages and few benefits for workers. Prostitution also thrives in this male dominant society, a fact I became acutely and embarrassingly aware of during my visit.

I met a young British woman named Amanda on my first foray into China. At that time, I spoke no Chinese and she took pity on me, teaming up with me to travel from China, through Macau to Hong Kong. We arrived in Macau late one evening and set out looking for an inexpensive place to spend the night. We went from place to place, with Amanda attempting to bargain with the concierge only to find the budget places full. Finally we found a place for 200 patacas, or about $20 U.S. The room was a dormer atop the roof. There were several other similar rooms on the roof and Amanda and I noticed a lot of traffic during the night. It seems these rooms are usually let by the hour to, shall we say, transitory trade. The next day I noticed that several of the large tourist hotels offered special rates for shower or steam bath and massage, which sounded like a real treat to me after roughing it in China for two weeks. Upon inquiring, I was met with incredulous expressions and told these services were only for men. I was determined, however, and set out to find such services for myself, leaving a message to that effect for Amanda, who had gone out. When she returned, she had a chat with the concierge that provided rich material for a classic book on miscommunication. I should point out that Amanda speaks Mandarin Chinese and the gentleman spoke some other dialect. It is not impossible, only rather difficult to bridge this gap, especially in the subtleties. Thinking that the concierge would know who offered massage for women, Amanda sought his advice on my behalf. At first he assumed I wanted "clients" for massage. When Amanda quickly assured him that this was not the case, he offered his own "services", wanting to know how much I would pay. All of this with a wink and a nudge. Fortunately, I was able to find a masseuse without his assistance.

It is easy and cheap to reach from Hong Kong where your housing prospects are much better. Generally, I would recommend that you go to Macau as a day trip. Very little is cheap in Macau, as it is a playground for rich men from all over Asia. Lately, Japanese tourists are flooding the island resulting in a number of very popular Karaoke bars.

Eating in Macau

Although the population is mostly Chinese, the names of the streets are mostly written in Chinese and Portuguese. There are also quite a few excellent restaurants reflecting Macau's cosmopolitan heritage. You will find dishes from Africa, Brazil, Portugal and, of course, China. The cuisine of these diverse cultures has been adapted to the local palate, making it uniquely Macanese and wonderfully tasty.

As you would expect in a seaport, many of these specialize in fish dishes. There are lots of little seafood places where you select your meal from a tank at the front of the shop. Macau is especially famous for baked crab, and grilled, stuffed king prawns. None of these restaurants are cheap; but if you include Macau in your itinerary, you absolutely must plan on a little mealtime extravagance. I promise you it's worth it.

Section Three

Some General Tips for the Budget Traveler

Packing for your Trip

When packing for your trip, keep your destination in mind. Are you going to a city or the countryside? The beach or the mountains? Going to a hot or cold climate? Asia? Europe? South America? Alaska? What kind of activities do you plan? Are you traveling to an Islamic country? If so, a modest wardrobe will be required. If you are headed to the beaches of Fiji or Ko Samui, a bathing suit is a must, but leave your fur at home. Hiking, backpacking and other athletic activities require a different sort of wardrobe than would be required for dancing or attending the ballet or opera. I prefer casual clothing but nearly always bring one outfit that will be acceptable for a dressier occasion, taking care that this ensemble is lightweight and totally wrinkle resistant. Duration of your stay is an equally important consideration. Some generalities do apply.

Rules 1 through 999 - Always Travel Light

So as to be ready to go at a moment's notice, I always keep my bag pre-packed with the following items:

Toothbrush, sample-size hotel soaps, deodorant, mouthwash and toothpaste, toilet tissue, SPF 30 (or greater) Sun Block, insect-repellant and small sewing kit, baby powder and travel wipes, comb and brush, water purification tablets, Swiss army knife, a pair of chopsticks, medical kit with Benadryl Cream, Ibuprofen (Motrin or equivalent), alcohol swabs and Bandaids.

Most people pack way too much and, as a consequence, are overburdened while traveling. For a two-week stay in a tropical climate, I take the following clothing:

Five sets of underwear, three pair of shorts (two pair running shorts, one pair walking shorts) Three light-weight tee shirts and one wrinkle-resistant blouse. One crushable dress and one wrinkle-resistant skirt. One bathing suit, one phaasin (the all-purpose wrap purchased in Chiang Mai) One sun visor or cloth baseball-type cap and sunglasses for sun protection. One pair each, running shoes, walking shoes and sandals.

I have actually traveled for a month with a backpack containing only the items listed above. All fabrics should be lightweight and drip-dry, easy to rinse out and dry overnight. I always bring a lightweight clothesline and clips to facilitate the task.

When visiting a cold climate, I wear a lightweight Gortex ski suit or other warm travel clothes and pack the following clothing:

Two sets of Thermal underwear in addition to underwear previously listed
Two pair running tights, one light-weight, one thermal
Three long-sleeved tee shirts and one long-sleeved sweater
Stocking cap and polypropylene gloves
Running shoes and walking shoes

In a rainy climate you may want to include a collapsible umbrella or one of those emergency rain parkas that fold into a tiny plastic pouch. Personally, I don't mind getting wet and rarely use an umbrella. In the tropics, people often use umbrellas for protection from the sun and, being fair-skinned, I should put an umbrella to this use. I must confess to being negligent in this regard.

I also take writing supplies (as a writer, I take my laptop and extra disks, but you should definately take a tablet to use as a trip journal) a daypack for short side trips, a small calculator, a guidebook appropriate to the area, such as one of the Travel Survival Kit series, a traveller's guide to the language and a novel to read while resting or waiting for transport. All of these things can be carried in one soft-sided suitcase suitable for use as carry-on baggage when flying.

At first I always took a camera and film, but later came to realize I was spending an inordinate amount of time and money getting pictures and developing them. I was also concerned about losing my camera. Now I rarely take it with me. It's much easier and cheaper to purchase scenic views wherever I go and there is one less thing to worry about.

If you feel naked without one, I recommend bringing a simple, cheap, utilitarian camera without accessories. You might profit by purchasing both camera and film on a trip to Asia, as these commodities are relatively inexpensive there.

Monetary Matters

Obtaining foreign currency

Whenever planning a trip, watch the fluctuation of the dollar in the prospective country. Big city newspapers and the Wall Street Journal list the major currencies. If the dollar is falling relative to the currency required, I always order a good supply through my bank, which can take up to two weeks. If the dollar is stable versus the foreign currency, I send for enough for ground transportation, two meals and a hotel stay for the first night. Because of the frequency of my travels; I never turn exchange money before going home. In this way I always have a small cache to tide me over the first day or so.

In countries where moneychangers or the black market will give you a better deal than the official currency, take enough for one day and night. Hong Kong and Singapore are in this category. Thailand apparently has no black market for currency. I was able to profit buying British Pounds before going, as the value of the dollar was declining in Britain at that time. Currently the situation has reversed and it would pay to wait. Thailand and China do not allow travellers to bring large amounts of their currency into their countries. I purchase Malay, Chinese or Thai currency after entering each country.

Most banks and moneychangers charge a premium of some kind. When you inquire about exchange rates, always find out if the amount quoted includes any fee. Sometimes they will quote a much better rate that the current official amount and then tack on an exchange premium. Many charge an extra premium for traveller's checks and you will find that some will give a more favorable rate for a larger sum of money. ATM's may prove to be the best alternative, giving the most favorable rate of exchange for a minimal fee. When using ATM's, the fee is charged per transaction, usually $1.50 to $2.50, so it would be best to get as much as you think you will need in one fell swoop.

In China, there is a dual monetary system. Foreigners are supposed to trade in Foreign Exchange Certificates, or FEC, while residents trade in Renminbi (literally translated, peoples money) or RMB. Tourist hotel bookings, restaurants and transportation must be purchased with FEC's. Local transportation and youth hostels dai pai dongs and small merchants may be paid with RMB, although they are always thrilled to get FEC. Chinese nationals covet may foreign items which can only be bought with FEC, which results in a brisk black market trade. RMB is traded at a favorable rate relative to the FEC, so it is worth your while to do some money swapping. It is entirely legal. Don't worry about finding a RMB dealer, he will find you. Watch out for the con artists who count the RMB while it is folded double. The count can be nearly doubled in this manner. Before you turn over any FEC, have the RMB counted bill by bill into your hand.

I encountered this same practice in Malaysia when trading Singapore dollars for Malaysian. Official moneychangers and banks post their rates and appear to be scrupulous. It is a good idea to ask for advice on changing money at your youth hostel. In Singapore and China moneychangers give you a better deal than the banks.

A money belt is probably a good idea, especially if there is room in it for important documents such as passport and return air ticket. In general you will find pickpockets wherever there are crowds in any country.

Never, ever pack cash in your suitcase. No airline will assume responsibility for the loss of cash in stowed baggage; and you might lose everything. Early in this book I related an incident in which my bag did not go to the airport with me. It would have been a complete disaster if I had packed my money, as I had to purchase everything I needed while away.

Using Credit Cards

You will doubtless find in some areas that all your bargaining comes to naught when you present your credit card as payment.

At the very least the merchant will add about 6% to the tab. You may want to consider reserving your credit cards for special purchases which merit insurance against loss, theft or fraud. You can use your credit card to get cash in an emergency, but it will cost more than usual, as you will pay interest daily from the date of the transaction. If you need cash, use your ATM and you will get the best available exchange rate. Do bear in mind that most lending institutions charge an extra premium if you use your ATM card at non-member banks and at banks in foreign countries.

The advantages of using your credit card are basically four:
1. Your purchases are automatically insured against loss or theft.
2. You will automatically be charged the most favorable rate of exchange.
3. You will have a record of your purchases.
4. If your cash is lost or stolen, you are out of luck, but a credit card (or traveler's checks) can be replaced within 24 hours no matter where you are.

How Much Money Shall I Bring?

Since I nearly always spend whatever I bring along, I deal with that question by calculating beforehand how much I will need, then adding twenty percent for extravagance and emergency. I can easily get by on about $200 for two weeks in Hong Kong, less in China, Malaysia or Thailand and a little more in Singapore. Great Britain costs about $300 per week, with San Francisco, New York, Los Angeles, Greece, Italy, Spain and other regions approximately $250. This allows for housing, food, ground transportation and inexpensive souvenirs. On a month-long sojourn in China, I spent a total of $635 including air fare. In the interest of full disclosure, I must admit this was a short notice flight, and the air fare cost only $50 round trip!

I spend more on those trips when I purchase Christmas presents for my family. In Asia, I purchase clothing, toys, books, electronics, leather goods and jewelry at considerable savings, from 30 to 50% less than the best sale prices at home. Bargains in leather goods, artwork and clothing are abundant in Italy. In New York you can find almost anything you want to buy at bargain rates, but be careful about quality and don't buy jewelry from individuals who solicit on the streets in New York City. These people capitalize on our natural greedy impulse to get a hot bargain. Most buyers assume that maybe the merchandise is "hot" or that the seller is avoiding taxes, but just remember, that the gold probably isn't.

I have also learned of a scam where they approach you from a van, offering electronic equipment at rock bottom prices. The con artists entice you, showing you a display sample of working merchandise, but once they get your money, they'll give you an apparently unopened box. It won't contain anything like the sample. Caveat emptor!

Illness

Most countries offer heavily subsidized or socialized medical care. If you become ill, your best bet is to head for a government hospital. They usually charge very little or nothing. If you elect to consult a private clinic you will still pay less than you would in the United States.

Check with your insurance agent before you travel in your own or any other country. Ask about procedure and documentation for reimbursement. Many countries accept a Blue Cross or other major Insurance card as proof of coverage, but most will insist on pre-payment. This is one case in which you will want to use your credit card for purposes of obtaining precise documentation. If you charge your tickets on your card, you will automatically be insured against death or accidents while travelling.

A lot of illness can be prevented by taking simple precautions. Wash your hands frequently with warm, soapy water and keep them away from your face. We transmit most viruses and bacteria into our bodies with our hands. Avoid crowds when possible. In Japan, sick people who must go out publicly wear masks to protect others. Perhaps the rest of the world will eventually adopt this considerate and civilized practice!

Don't drink the water unless you are certain it is safe, no matter where you are travelling. There have been outbreaks of chryptosporidium and giardia nearly everywhere in the world. My own experience with these nasty bugs came when I got lost while running in the mountains near my home on a hot summer day. Concerned about dehydration, I drank from several creeks on my search for the trail. I thought it would be safe because I had read somewhere that if water is cold, clear and fast running, it's okay. Oops! Take it from me, you can become very sick from these organisms. Do bear in mind that some offending bacteria can survive freezing, so it is wise to avoid ice cubes in your beverages. Avoid meats and seafoods except in first class restaurants with obvious high sanitation standards.

Some people include anti-diarrheals and antacid preparations in their medical kit. As a rule, I find that you can buy the same preparations in Asia or Mexico for less, so in those areas I buy them only if and when needed. China is a notable exception to the Asian principle. I never found an apothecary or drug store in any of the smaller towns or villages, so I carry those medications when trekking in China.

Always bring some kind of antiseptic and bandaids for cuts, blisters and scrapes. You may find sanitation less than ideal and you will want to avoid infection. Cortisone cream is useful for rashes and burns and I like a topical cream which combines anti-pyretic, antipruretic, antibacterial and antiseptic properties. Ask your druggist for advice.

If you suffer from motion sickness, try 1000 to 1500 mg of ginger (available in health food stores) half an hour before traveling. The Chinese have used this with remarkable success for centuries and there are no known side effects, such as the sleepiness you get with prescription drugs. If you prefer you can swig ginger ale, especially the concentrated variety you'll find in health food stores.

Lately there has been heartening news from the medical profession suggesting that you can ward off some common traveller's illnesses by consuming red wine. Apparently there are antibiotic properties in the wine which have been recognized for centuries, and medicine now agrees that it might be helpful. Overindulgence, however, may cause more problems that it will prevent.

The Dreaded Jet Lag

No discussion of travel afflictions would be complete without mention of jet lag. You will hear people complaining about jet lag on a three or four hour trip. I've had no personal experience with jet lag on short flights, but believe me, on a twelve hour or longer flight, it can be a real problem. Upon return from my first Asian trip I was ill for nearly two weeks.

After that experience, I purchased a book which promised prevention of jet lag . The book jacket blurb proclaimed that the method had worked for world travellers and diplomats such as Henry Kissinger. Basically, this was a high protein, low carbohydrate dietary approach which would be difficult if not impossible for a vegetarian. I did manage, with difficulty, to follow the program, but it was ineffective for me. Since then, I have devised my own method of dealing with time changes and long flights. It works very well for me, so I'm including it here for your information and use:

1. While airborne, drink a lot of water and fruit juice as flying is dehydrating.
2. Forget the movie and sleep as much as possible on the flight.
3. Avoid alcoholic beverages on the flight, as alcohol is dehydrating.
4. When you arrive at your destination, immediately adapt to the time zone. This means go to sleep if it is nighttime. Go sightseeing or for a walk or a run if it's day time, getting as much sun as possible. Try to stay awake until it is time to sleep, then sleep for your usual eight hours.
5. When you go home, repeat rule 1, 2 and 3. Sleep around the clock or stay in bed 24 to 36 hours, then adapt to time zone, getting as much sunlight during the daytime as possible.

I have found this method quite successful and rarely suffer from jet lag these days, unless I am unable to comply with rule 4. When that happens, I'm usually headachy and a little sick for about a week. Whatever you else you do, be careful to drink a lot of fluids (and I don't mean alcohol, which will dehydrate you). I am reasonably certain that dehydration contributes significantly to jet lag. I have also come to believe that jet lag has a detrimental effect on the immune system. I've noted that upon return from a long trip, I seem to lack my customary resistance to disease and occasionally become ill. I am ordinarily resistant to such illness, thanks to a healthy immune system, which I supplement with echinacea when under stress.

Lately, there has been a great deal in the media about the use of melatonin in combating jet lag. Scientific studies seem to back up this use, and it seems worth a try and I have found no medical reports of remarkable side effects. Apparently it works by re-setting your internal clock. Check this out at the health food store.

It is generally unwise to fly when you have an upper respiratory tract infection. The same phenomenon that causes your ears to "pop" can result in a nasty ear infection. Should the occasion arise when you must fly under these circumstances, be sure to obtain a good nasal decongestant and use it before and during the flight.

Safety and Security

Safety is an important consideration wherever you travel. With all the frightening media accounts of foreign tourists being targeted in Florida, one could easily conclude that the whole of the United States is a difficult and dangerous place for a visitor. To put this in proper perspective, one should be mindful of the truly staggering number of tourists who travel unmolested in America and elsewhere every day of every year. Any place can be dangerous, even one's own back yard. Statistically, the most dangerous activity in the United States is driving an automobile; but few would give up the convenience and economy of driving.

There have been growing concerns about terrorism worldwide, giving rise to extra precautions when flying or visiting many areas of the world. There are precautions one can take to assure a reasonably safe trip at home or anywhere. My safety rules are as follows:

1. Get the State Department Booklet entitled "Know Before You Go" and follow the advice within. If there is a State Department Advisory against travel to a given area, don't go there. If in doubt about the safety of a specific area due to political or criminal activity, your congressional office is a great source of the latest information. You will find a local telephone number listed in your directory.

2. Regardless of your destination, be observant. Keep your eyes open and report irregularities such as unattended baggage or packages wherever you see them - in airport terminals, busy streets or places where crowds gather. It's certainly better to be safe than sorry, and no one will fault you for reporting an innocent package.

3. Keep your valuables on your person whenever possible. Better yet, don't take anything with you that you cannot afford to lose. Some hotels will insist on keeping your passport during your stay, but I generally refuse to let it out of my possession unless there is absolutely no choice. There is a huge black market demand for American passports, especially in Hong Kong and China. Just to be on the safe side, memorize and then record your passport number, date and place of issuance and expiration date in your travel diary or some other trustworthy place. Should you lose your travel documents, go to the nearest embassy or consulate representing your country and they will assist you.

4. Do not flash a large amount of money in public. Keep small amounts handy for routine purchases. Money belts are better for significant amounts of money and travel documents. You're most likely to get your pocket picked in crowds, such as bus or train travel. Be aware of any attempt to divert your attention and don't let go of your own bags to assist others.

5. Young women should be wary of men offering jobs. Do not get into a vehicle with any stranger. If you want work, agree

to meet the prospective employer at the work site or some other public place. Notify police and consulate of your whereabouts, explaining the circumstances. Take someone with you if possible. Also, thoroughly check out the locks of your hotel rooms and check the walls for peep holes. I have heard some stories in Thailand that necessitate the latter precaution. Don't take in the night life alone. You can always find several others in your hostel who want to tour the city at night and check out the pubs and nightclubs. Avoid alcohol in less than totally secure surroundings. Drinking alcoholic beverages, even small amounts, can cloud your judgment.

6. A few years ago I read some discouraging stories about young backpackers in Australia, both male and female, being murdered by a serial killer. The victims were all trekking in the Australian outback, and in at least one case the victims were a couple travelling together. The killer was eventually caught when one abductee broke away. It can't hurt to read the newspapers from any area you are planning to visit to see what's going on. If you have questions about the area once there, check with the local police for their safety recommendations.

7. Consider purchasing a personal alarm device. These are usually quite small and can be activated by pulling a tab or string. Once activated, they make a lot of noise and draw attention to your situation. I've seen these alarms priced from $5 and up at AAA travel stores and other shops specializing in travel. The luggage department of any store is a good place to look.

8. If you are travelling to a remote area alone, consider teaming up with several other people who are headed in the same direction. Youth hostels are great places for meeting like-minded travelers and you can get to know them first. Leave word of your travel plans with your embassy or consulate and let your prospective travelling companions know that you are doing it

9. Here's one I learned the hard way. If you have to undergo a physical check at an airport security point, don't take your eyes off the belongings that are going through x-ray. There are airport thieves who watch for travellers whose attention is diverted. While you aren't watching your stuff, they walk away with purses and wallets left on the x-ray belt. The security staff is no help here. My wallet was lifted this way in San Francisco with $300 in it. Fortunately the wallet was left in a rest room, minus the cash - but credit cards, passport and other I.D. intact.

Some General Considerations

Solo Travel or Teaming up

Shall I travel solo or find travel companions? I cannot answer that one for you as the right response depends heavily upon one's personal preferences. I offer for your contemplation the following list of comparative benefits:

Solo	Accompanied
Change plans on a whim	Fresh ideas on travel plans
Enjoy solitude when desired	Enjoy companionship
Indulge in favorite solo activities	Share great experiences
Total independence, freedom	Share housing expenses
Total control of daily expenses	Help in illness or emergency
Travel at your own pace	General Safety

As you can see, there are benefits and penalties either way. I compromise and team up when circumstances warrant, striking out on my own when so moved. The best possible situation is finding a companion who likes the same things and respects your need for solitude. I find that if these considerations are fully discussed and agreed upon beforehand, you are likely to have a pleasant journey. This practice has resulted in a lot of fun times and a few very special and lasting friendships.

Best Times to Travel

When flying as a courier, airfares are not appreciably affected by peak or off-peak rates so cost is not a usually a factor in choosing travel time. I prefer to travel to non-tropical areas when the weather is warm. This is not a matter of enjoying warm versus cold climate; rather it is a reflection of the amount of gear you need to pack. I am also fond of visiting the tropics when it is winter at home. This seems to foster greater appreciation of both places! Personally, I love going to Asian destinations during special festivals such as Chinese New Year. Weather notwithstanding, you can't beat Times Square in New York on New Year's Eve! New York is really magical during the holidays, especially when there's snow on the ground.

Of course you will want to take advantage of special promotions when they occur, which requires flexibility in your travel plans. These offers usually emerge during off-season when airlines want to fill seats. When you see an especially good promotion, call right away, bearing in mind that such offers are always limited and are frequently withdrawn without notice.

Appendix A: Air Courier Companies

Please note that some of these companies have downsized, resulting in fewer central booking offices. Because of this, if you wish to fly out of San Francisco, for example, you may have to contact a Los Angeles or New York office. Also, the courier business is dynamic and you may find great fluctuations in policies and pricing, but this list will get you started. Please note that most large cities of the world will have offices of the major courier companies, even though they are not listed below, Halbart, Polo and Jupiter, in particular, have offices nearly everywhere in the world. If you don't find your country represented below, consult your telephone directory, read the advertisements in the newspapers and check with major airports in your area.

Company Location and Telephone
Able AirLondon(071)639-7563Able Travel & ToursNew York(212)779-8530
Air FacilitiesNew York(718)712-0630
Air Hitch   New York(212)864-2000
Los Angeles(310)485-1006
Bridges WorldwideNew York(718)244-7244
     Los Angelescall New York
     San Franciscocall New York
     London(081)759 5040
     Hong Kong852 2305 1412
              British Airways TravelLondon(081)754 1234
         Courier Network (Israel)New York(800)222-9951
Courier Travel ServicesLondon(071)351-0300
Discount Travel InternationalNew York(212)362-3636

Miami(305)593-0260
FB On-Board CourierLondon(0753)680280
Toronto(416)675-1820
Montreal(514)633-0740
Vancouver(604)278-1266
Halbart Express New York(718)656-8189
Chicago(708)409-1600
Miami(305)593-1616
IBCLos Angeles(310)607-0125

Jupiter AirAustralia   (61)(2)666 4655
Germany   (49)(69)6902833
Hong Kong(852)(03)7351886
Japan   (81)(03)444-6771
 London(081)751-3323
New York(718)656-6050
Los Angeles(310)670-5123
San Francisco(415)697-1773
Line Haul ServicesMiami(305)477-0651
Now Voyager New York(212)431-1616
Houstoncall New York
Miamicall New YorkPolo Express London(081)759-5383
Los Angeles(310)410-6822
UTLSan Francisco(415)583-5074
Way to Go TravelLos Angeles(213)466-1126
San Diego(619)224-2277

Appendix B

Budget Travel Guides

Most of these publications are available at your local library (Free, folks!) and if they aren't, make a request. Most libraries will attempt to obtain the publications you are interested in reading.

Consumer Reports Travel Letter
Send $39 to Subscription Department
P.O.Box 51366, Boulder Colorado 80321

The Courier Air Travel Handbook by Mark I. Field
Thunderbird Press, 5930-10 W. Greenway Rd. #112B
Glendale, Arizona 85306

Insiders Guide to Air Courier Bargains by Kelly Monaghan
Send $14.95 to Inwood Training Publications
Box 438, New York, N.Y. 10034

International Youth Hostel Federation Publications
Purchase through your local Hostelling organization

Jim's Backpacker's Bible
Purchase at independent hostels or send check or money order as follows:

North America (including Hawaii) $6.00 per copy
International orders $7.00 per copy, check payable to Jim's Backpacker's Bible, P.O. Box 5650, Santa Monica, CA 90409

The Travel Unlimited Newsletter
$25 Subscription to Steve Lantos
P.O. Box 1058, Allstone, MA 02134

US and Worldwide Travel Accommodations Guide
Mail Check for $12.95 to Campus Travel Service, P.O. Box 5007, Laguna Beach, Ca. 92652

See your local library for the following publications:

The Travel Survival Kit to... series, North-East Asia On a Shoestring and other "On a Shoestring" series and other guides put out by Lonely Planet Publications, P.O. Box 617, Hawthorne, Victoria 3122, Australia, U.S. office, P.O. Box 2001A, Berkeley, CA 94702 or go the the Lonely Planet website at http://www.lonelyplanet.com.

Passport to Discount Travel by Christopher Allen

Sanctuaries, The West Coast and Southwest, Marcia and Jack Kelly

Vagabonding in the USA: A Guide to Independent Travel

Write to the author:

Your comments and suggestions for future editions are more than welcome. If there is a destination not covered in the book, or you want the latest information on anywhere, please let me hear from you and I'll do my best to accommodate your needs. You can contact me via e-mail at gomh@aol.com, or write: Maureen A. Hennessy 1090 Ellendale Drive D15, Medford, Oregon 97504.

Printed in the United States
210018BV00001B/34-36/A

9 781893 652491